The Power of Generosity

Dave Toycen

The Power of Generosity

How to Transform Yourself
and Your World

HarperCollins*PublishersLtd*

The Power of Generosity
© 2004, 2005 by Dave Toycen. All rights reserved.

Published by HarperCollins Publishers Ltd

"Am I Greedy?" Appendix C, is adapted and reprinted with permission
from *The Sin of Greed and the Spirit of Generosity* by Robert C. Roberts,
Center for Applied Christian Ethics, Wheaton College, 1994.

First hardcover edition by HarperCollins Publishers Ltd: 2004
This trade paperback edition with new preface: 2005

HarperCollins books may be purchased for educational, business,
or sales promotional use through our Special Markets Department.

HarperCollins Publishers Ltd
2 Bloor Street East, 20th Floor
Toronto, Ontario, Canada
M4W 1A8

www.harpercollins.ca

Library and Archives Canada Cataloguing in Publication

Toycen, Dave
The power of generosity : how to transform yourself
and the world / Dave Toycen. – 1st trade pbk. ed.

Includes bibliographical references.
ISBN-13: 978-0-00-639439-6
ISBN-10: 0-00-639439-6

1. Generosity. I. Title.

BJ1533.G4T68 2005   177'.7   C2004-907068-1

HC 9 8 7 6 5 4

Printed and bound in the United States
Set in Monotype Perpetua

To my parents, LaVerne and Elaine Toycen, who taught me to love people and follow Jesus, and to my wife, Diane, who practises generosity every day.

Contents

Preface

Why have I written a book about generosity? In a world of grinding poverty and humanitarian crisis, people of action are needed—people who have had enough of words. In many cases words themselves have betrayed those who suffer. From the expansive declarations of increasing aid to developing countries to the past promises of humanitarian intervention in places such as Rwanda and the Democratic Republic of the Congo, the poor have experienced the lack of real commitment behind all the talk. Words of promise and hope have been so compromised that they sometimes result in more chaos.

But there is another possibility. Words can still convey aspiration and encouragement.

I knew this was true in the days right after the Boxing Day tsunami of 2004—the worst natural disaster in living memory—when I walked among ruined homes and agonized with bereaved parents and orphaned children. Even as I grieved with these survivors, I was moved and challenged by the outpouring of generosity from people both inside and outside the crisis zone. For a few days, we were a global community, setting aside ethnic, political and cultural differences, on a shared mission to save lives.

I met Sharmila Croos, a mother from Sri Lanka, who lost absolutely everything, but whose family was spared. She assured me that her family could manage, and urged me to tell Canadians to focus their giving on people who have lost children and relatives instead.

And so it went: a 90-year-old Saudi millionaire who was so concerned that he travelled to Indonesia to see the damage firsthand, gave $12 million to help build new homes in Banda Aceh. A father in his thirties who lost his wife and two children in the tsunami was acting as a guard at one of our children's centres in Indonesia. He shared with me that he was overwhelmed with grief but he was somehow finding meaning in work that was helping children. And a mother in India who lost three of her four children spoke, through her tears, of her faith and of how God's mercy was sustaining her.

I have written this book about generosity to tell something of those who suffer and those who triumph. Frequently they are one and the same. In spite of horrifying circumstances that threaten to take their lives, these people continue to live with generosity and compassion. As an aid worker, it is humbling to see such courage and perseverance in the midst of circumstances that grind the hope out of living. This is the real truth of mothers and fathers and children who have next to nothing except the dignity of their humanity and an indomitable spirit. Amazingly, many of them still believe in God and they make a clear distinction between what people do to each other and how God might be responsible. They are long on patience and high on faith.

In contrast to our consumer mentality that insists "you are what you own," this book celebrates the millions of people who practise generosity daily. We need more like them. They are a shining light in the broader context of human need that stretches around the globe.

We were created to be generous. I am convinced of it. Scientists are beginning to find evidence that we're programmed to help each other, but most of us have known it in our hearts for a long time.

I have been most fortunate to be around truly generous people. Most of them behaved generously with a lack of pretension that made their giving more powerful. My grandparents, father, mother, aunts and uncles were wonderful people who gave generously and often. You will meet some of them in this book. Some of my greatest teachers have also been women and men living in developing countries. In the midst of unimaginable suffering and neglect, they practise generosity as if it is the air they breathe. You will meet some of them too.

Mostly this book is about the joy of giving and the difference it can make. I hope and pray you will find something that lifts your heart and sustains your spirit so that together we can build a future for ourselves and our children. Time is short but the opportunities are endless.

DAVE TOYCEN
March 2005

Acknowledgments

I have been blessed with so many people who have enriched my life and encouraged my understanding of generosity. In addition to my parents and my wife, I have been blessed with a family that truly cares—my three siblings, my two children, grandparents, aunts and uncles and cousins. The list goes on and on.

In my professional life, numerous leaders and colleagues at World Vision have enlivened my perspective and offered examples that have made all the difference: Graeme Irvine, Stan Mooneyham, Ed Dayton and Ted Engstrom in the United States; Bill Newell, Don Scott and Linda Tripp in Canada;

Acknowledgments

Harold Henderson, Warwick Olson, Philip Hunt and John Rose in Australia; Manfred Grellert in Latin America; and Wilfred Mlay in Africa.

The pastors of three outstanding churches have stimulated and challenged my religious life— George Regas in the United States, Peter Corney in Australia and Harold Percy in Canada.

I would like to express appreciation for the example and influence of the late Lewis Smedes, one of my professors at Fuller Theological Seminary, whose unconditional commitment to hope and thoughtful caring helped me move beyond the parochial nature of my earlier understanding. The late Bruce Gyngell, television guru extraordinaire, was my mentor in connecting executive leadership with a passionate, vulnerable regard for people.

Thanks to my friend Tom Cochrane, who is generous to the cause of children and an unfailing encourager.

Perhaps most important are the numerous families in poor countries who have taken me into their lives as a stranger and shared generously of their life experience. If there is anything in this book that is helpful, then it comes from them. I am humbled by the nameless persons around the world who have given their lives to live generously when their circumstances were unjust and oppressive.

Acknowledgments

This book would never have happened without the writing support and research from Marla Stewart Konrad, my communications advisor. My executive assistant, Caroline Sokoloski, provided the coordination and office support that gave the time and privacy to do the writing. Chris Bucci, my editor at HarperCollins, was helpful, patient and wonderfully professional. The same can be said of Shona Cook and the rest of the team at Harper Collins. Researcher Karen Stiller and editor Don Loney made essential contributions to begin the dream.

Finally, the board and corporation of World Vision Canada has been generous in their encouragement of this project. They represent the tens of thousands of World Vision supporters whose generosity inspires me every day.

In the end, in spite of the best counsellors and advisors, any mistakes that might appear are mine. My primary solace is that there are far fewer than when we started this enterprise.

"We make a living by what we get, but we make a life by what we give."

(Norman MacEwan)

Chapter One

Generosity: What Is It?

Generosity has been an important idea to me for a long time. Yet it was on a warm summer day in August 1997 in Sand Creek, Wisconsin, that its importance gained new meaning. It was my father's funeral. The sunshine was intermittent with thick cumulus clouds floating across the sky. The country church was packed with more than 400 people paying their respects. A steady line-up of local farm folk streamed by the casket. There were the many gestures of respect, handshakes, a pat on the shoulder, a tear. Some spoke about my father, of his enthusiasm, his willingness to lend a hand, the numerous times he provided financial assistance and his frequent visits to those who were sick and dying. My sister Gail and I spoke with laughter and humour of this man who was filled with generosity and enthusiasm. Dad's first cousin, now an elderly man in his early eighties, described him as a person who had "the gift of helps"—a rather old-fashioned way to describe behaviour that constantly reaches out to benefit others.

There was a sombre quality to this day, but it was also a day of celebration, and the memories of my father prompted the final decision to write this book. His life was the conclusive reminder to me that the journey of generosity is a story worth telling.

I am one of those fortunate people who grew up with a father who was generous, at times to a fault. My brother, who was in business with our dad for more than twenty years, told me, "Dad cried about people, but he never cried about money." Practically, it meant that money took second place to people. He had a caring heart. So often Dad would buy more than he needed so he could give some away. If buying one was good, then two was twice as good and three would be ten times better. It wasn't necessarily good economics, but it was great generosity.

When returning from a trip to a larger city, Dad would arrive loaded down with fruit and vegetables that were less available in our area. They would be distributed to family, staff at his car dealership and farm, and of course friends along the way. He had a special joy in sharing with someone who was having difficulty of some kind. My dad had learned a great secret: giving generously is a wonderful way to live. The crowd paying tribute to my father that day was the exclamation point at the end of a fantastic life.

My father's gift of helps was a testimony to me that our attitude toward others is an essential part of our epitaph. If you lead a good life, you are assured a good death. This doesn't mean that your death will not be tragic, but your memory and, more importantly, your heritage will be passed along to the generations that follow. Generosity has the power to leave a legacy of goodwill.

There are a number of virtues that shape our response to the needs of others. It would be simplistic and naive to insist that generosity is the only one that matters. Philosopher Tibor Machan comments, "while generosity is on the whole a virtue, it needs to coexist with other virtues to lead one to act ethically, that is, to be good on the whole."[1] For example, a person could be generous in dispensing contributions to various charities, yet his business practices are corrupt and unjust. His generosity toward charity presents a misleading picture of his real character. Compassion, charity, duty and justice are all important virtues as we interact with one another. In fact they should all work in harmony. I've chosen generosity as the topic of this book because I believe it touches every relationship on a daily basis. It is the lubricant that smoothes our daily living in a way that affects every other moral virtue. In fact, I believe that generosity is the first car in the train of virtues. Without it, the other virtues are unlikely to ever get started or be fully expressed.

On a number of occasions I have observed individuals who wish to practise charity, but their attitude is so lacking in generosity that the expression of charity is almost lost. There is such precision and calculation to their gift that one questions whether they really mean to help another person or simply check off another mark on the list of good things they have to do. In an unfortunate way the process of expressing their charity undermines the very wholesomeness of the virtue. Generosity removes the pettiness and calculation that can easily work against the goodness of our original intent. The Bible describes the attitude that the giver should practise when making a contribution—don't let the left hand know what the right hand is doing. (Matthew 6:3) The implication is not to think too much about your gift or how it will benefit you. The gift that is too calculated is not worth giving.

Living at a time when our society is beleaguered by materialism, generosity is an essential medicine to combat the striving for more. Though it may not make the evening news, there is a huge reservoir of giving to others that sustains life. I believe it's a major factor in holding our fragile world together. From the willingness to forgive the terrible crimes of apartheid in South Africa to the generous out-pourings of contributions to daily food banks, there is another way. If you listen and look carefully you can find generosity in every community of our world.

During the conflict in Kosovo, I interviewed a ten-year-old boy named Liridan who had fled with his parents from the conflict to neighbouring Albania. While boarding a farm wagon in his local village to escape the invading soldiers, he was struck on the arm by a rifle butt. His arm was broken and, over the course of a harrowing three-day journey, Liridan lost consciousness, but in the end he made it to freedom. Now Liridan and his family were crowded together in a broken-down gymnasium with scores of other refugee families. There was little privacy, a shortage of water and putrid, overcrowded latrines. His mother wept as she described the terror of their ordeal, especially the fear that the soldiers would kill Liridan.

As the interview was coming to a conclusion, I noticed a small package of tin foil in Liridan's good hand. Earlier one of the church groups had distributed small Easter presents for the children—most of whom owned nothing now except the clothes on their backs. With a child's spontaneity this traumatized little boy opened his hand, peeled back the foil, broke a section of chocolate into two pieces and offered one to me. Liridan's gesture took me completely by surprise. I could only nod and express my appreciation. I felt so small before this selfless act of generosity.

The dictionary defines generous as "of a noble nature, willing to give or share; large, ample." The focus is on the free will nature of the gift, which contrasts with the duty-like quality of charity. In Western civilization, generosity has strong roots in the biblical concept of a Creator who offers life to humankind as a gift. God is not required to do this. Elsewhere in the Bible, the generous person is identified as someone to emulate. "Good will come to him who is generous and lends freely, who conducts his affairs with justice." (Psalm 112:5, NIV) Or "A generous man will himself be blessed, for he shares his food with the poor." (Proverbs 22:9, NIV)

Later, in the New Testament, Jesus holds up giving and generous people as examples. The story of the Good Samaritan still resonates as a model for the truly caring person.

On one occasion an expert in the law stood up to test Jesus. "Teacher," he asked, "what must I do to inherit eternal life?"

"What is written in the Law?" he replied. "How do you read it?"

He answered: "'Love the Lord your God with all your heart and with all your soul and with all your strength and with all your mind'; and, 'Love your neighbour as yourself.'"

"You have answered correctly," Jesus replied. "Do this and you will live."

But he wanted to justify himself, so he asked Jesus, "And who is my neighbour?" In reply Jesus said: "A man was going down from Jerusalem to Jericho, when he fell into the hands of robbers. They stripped him of his clothes, beat him and went away, leaving him half dead. A priest happened to be going down the same road, and when he saw the man, he passed by on the other side. So too, a Levite, when he came to the place and saw him, passed by on the other side. But a Samaritan, as he travelled, came where the man was; and when he saw him, he took pity on him. He went to him and bandaged his wounds, pouring on oil and wine. Then he put the man on his own donkey, took him to an inn and took care of him. The next day he took out two silver coins and gave them to the innkeeper. 'Look after him,' he said, 'and when I return, I will reimburse you for any extra expense you may have.'

"Which of these three do you think was a neighbour to the man who fell into the hands of robbers?" The expert in the law replied, "The one who had mercy on him." Jesus told him, "Go and do likewise." (Luke 10:25–37, NIV)

The twist in this particular story underscores the point that generosity is a simple act of caring. Your status in society and your particular beliefs take second place to how you behave toward others. Samaritans were considered inferior by the prevailing culture in which Jesus lived. Faithful followers of the mainline Jewish faith of the time considered them part of a cult that had fallen away from the true faith. Jesus identifies the Samaritan as the hero, the truly compassionate person, in contrast to those who are typically seen as more honourable and respected. Doing good transcends your particular group, doctrine or religious affiliation. This attitude is at the very heart of what it means to practise generosity, and part of the foundation for justice and tolerance in Western civilization. But generosity has a place in all major faith traditions.

In Islam, the faithful believer practises "sadaqah," which usually means voluntary almsgiving to support the poor in the community. However, it can refer to any act of kindness toward another person, or even animals. The emphasis is on giving freely, which contrasts with the mandated "zakat," a welfare religious tax required of believers. On numerous occasions I have experienced the generosity toward strangers practised by Muslims. Hospitality and care are generously offered without any expectation of payment or reward.

In Buddhism, there is an emphasis on doing the most compassionate thing. The intention is as important as the act of giving. Being generous out of a desire to gain public admiration will hinder spiritual growth. The priority is to practise compassion without a desire for recognition or applause. Care for others reflects the commitment to follow the Eightfold Path of Buddhism, which in turn is said to provide a way to end the cravings and pleasures of this life. Following this philosophy it appears that generosity is strongly connected to the practice of compassion.[2]

Generosity need not be complicated or demanding. Often it's very simple gestures that make the difference. Raymond Chan, formerly Canada's Secretary of State for Asia in the Chrétien government, told me the story of how he came to Canada with twenty dollars in his pocket. His sister had given him a job in her small shop in Vancouver. Each day he took the bus to work. One rainy day he was dressed in a coat and hat typical of Hong Kong. Raymond realized he would be recognized as a foreigner, and his inadequate knowledge of English frightened him.

Standing at the bus stop, two tall Canadian ladies were in conversation and Raymond was hoping against hope that they wouldn't notice him. To his dismay, one of them spoke to him and said, "Young man, where are you from?" In halting English, Raymond said, "I am from Hong Kong." Without hesitating, the lady reached out her hand and shook his, saying, "Welcome to Canada." Then, gesturing to him with a sweeping motion of her hand and pointing to the mountain landscape, she said, "Look around you. This is a big country and we need young, strong people like you to help us build it."

Tears came to Raymond's eyes as he told this story and re-lived the encouragement of those simple remarks. This woman will never know how her action prompted a young man to aspire to greatness in his adopted country. Her prompting was a significant factor in the life of a person who would be the first ethnic Chinese Canadian to be a member of federal cabinet. What she did was an act of kindness based on an attitude of generosity.

Reaching out to others is an approach to life that has tremendous implications. In my work at World Vision, I am truly amazed at the generous ways in which people give lavishly of their time and material means. Surprisingly, children are sometimes the most radical and committed. Children frequently forgo their birthday gifts in order to raise money to help those in need. Many children are the driving force to encourage their parents to sponsor a child overseas. One parent recently told me that her daughter works two hours every day, five days a week, to pay the thirty-three dollars per month to sponsor a child. This generous attitude in children, if nurtured and encouraged, will shape their inner moral voice for a lifetime.

But why are some people generous and others not? One church launched a study to determine what causes some members to be more generous than others. Much to the researchers' surprise, it was neither the cleverness of the church's appeals nor the power of the preaching. Instead, the most significant factor was whether the person had been taught generosity as a child. The impact of parents in teaching their children to give was the key that opened the world of giving. This is a powerful reminder to those of us who decry the lack of generosity today—what have we done to train our children in the ways of generosity?

Dr. Stephen Foster is a medical doctor, who, along with his family, has served for years in the African country of Angola. He is a third-generation member of a missionary family. Both his parents and grandparents instilled in Stephen the spirit of giving. Over the years, Stephen's medical practice in Angola has been overwhelmed by the realities of poverty, lack of education, government ineptitude and, on numerous occasions, civil war. Still, he believes in a different future for the people of Angola and has put his life, along with his family's, on the line. Why? He is a person of deep religious faith, and one of the consequences is an abiding generosity. Stephen has said, "Even when the times are tough, we must be prepared to speak the truth, call for justice and share compassion with those in need."

Stephen and his family remained in Angola in spite of the civil war that destroyed their work and facilities. After raising the funds to build a hospital on donated land, they are maintaining their partnership with the local people. Now that peace has come to Angola, his work has an even greater opportunity to bear fruit. Where does this generosity and commitment come from? Stephen, impassioned by his faith in God, is following the example set by his family over the previous two generations.

What difference does generosity really make in our daily lives and in our world today? Generosity is about relationship. It is a lubricant in our dealings with one another. The rough places are smoothed and the misunderstandings can be borne more patiently. Generous people have learned the truth that life's difficulties only grow in significance when we hold back what we have been given. Psychiatrist Karl Menninger once said that if you are feeling depressed, the best thing you can do is to cross to the other side of the tracks and help someone in need. Generosity has a healing effect on some of our deepest struggles.

In scientific studies we are discovering that giving and generosity are qualities that contribute to both emotional and physical health. Allan Luks, in his book *The Healing Power of Doing Good: The Health and*

Spiritual Benefit of Helping Others, surveyed more than 3,000 volunteers of all ages serving with twenty organizations. He documented what he calls a "helper's high." After performing a kind act, subjects described feelings of euphoria and calmness that countered their feelings of stress and tension. Luks summarized his findings with this comment, "Helping contributes to the maintenance of good health, and it can diminish the effect of diseases and disorders both serious and minor, psychological and physical."[3] Another study conducted in Tecumseh, Michigan, confirms that helping others will extend your life. The various physical, social and health activities of 2,700 men were surveyed over the course of ten years. Those who did regular volunteer work had death rates two and a half times lower than those who did not.[4]

In extreme situations, generosity can even save one's life. The Russian poet Irina Ratushinskaya describes what it was like to be held in the life-destroying conditions of a Soviet labour camp. She had been sentenced for anti-Soviet agitation and propaganda in her writing. Day after day the grind of prison life would remove almost every trace of what it meant to be a human being. The cold, the lack of clothing, the dreadful diet, malnutrition and illness conspired to reinforce each prisoner's lack of dignity and value. Irina writes about the inner life that, more than anything, sustained the prisoners in their survival.

"You must not," she writes, "under any circumstances, allow yourself to hate. Not because your tormentors have not earned it. But if you allow hatred to take root, it will flourish and spread during your years in the camps, driving out everything else, and ultimately corrode and warp your soul."[5] Instead, her bitter experiences taught her that the best way to retain one's own humanity was to care more about another's pain than your own. Sharing a precious scrap of bread or a piece of soap became a lifeline. A moment of conversation or a touch on the shoulder said, "I care." "We were not seeking to perform heroic acts; if anything, these were acts of self-preservation. Having lost the ability to see another's concerns before your own, you lose everything."[6] Generosity and care for others were two elements of humanity that the state could not destroy. To lose those was to lose everything. Being generous kept them alive.

Although it may result in personal benefit, generosity in its finest expression has a spontaneous quality. It appears genuine and lacks calculation. The biblical expression "God loves a cheerful giver" reminds us that giving alone is not enough. It should be accompanied by the right attitude. Generosity has the same requirement or it smacks of self-interest. By itself, the act of being generous in time, money or attention is not enough. True generosity is delivered in a package of humility, sensitivity and total regard for the other person.

In 1959 Drs. Reg and Catherine Hamlin took a break from their rewarding medical practice in Australia to go to Ethiopia to work among the poor. Their hearts so embraced the situation that, after a number of trips, they decided to stay. Their life's passion became helping women who had suffered tremendously during childbirth because of prolonged labour.

In Canada, doctors will call for a caesarean section if prolonged labour begins to threaten the mother or unborn child. In rural settings in countries like Ethiopia, women must labour until the end. In the most severe cases, the constant pressure of the baby's head creates a small fissure in the bladder called a fistula. Most often, the baby does not survive the arduous delivery. For the mother, a fistula causes permanent incontinence. The women who suffer through such a delivery, many of them teenagers, are consigned to a living hell. Since they cannot control their bladders they are shunned by their husbands and community and often left to live alone.

During a visit I paid to the Hamlins' clinic, Catherine described how these unfortunate women arrive by bus, donkey or on foot from across Ethiopia, hoping there might be some chance for them. I was introduced to a woman so ill and neglected that she arrived on her hands and knees. Catherine calls these victims of pain and discrimination "fistula pilgrims." The Hamlins fell in love with these women, and began to work with them, adapting a surgical technique that repairs the fistula and restores them to a normal life. Most are subsequently able to have other children.

It's a true miracle to see this wonderful outreach in action. The patient arrives wearing smelly clothes, eyes averted and obviously accustomed to abuse and rejection. She is ushered into a small but clean private office and offered a chair. Catherine, using an interpreter, explains what has happened during childbirth. She takes a white sheet of paper, uses her fist to represent the baby's head pushing against it until there is a hole in the paper. Then she takes a pitcher of water and pours it on the paper and shows how the water escapes through the small hole. Taking the same sheet of paper, she holds it up against the glass windowpane and explains how a simple operation will repair it. During this time the flap of paper has re-adhered to the sheet and

Catherine shows the patient how everything will be restored.

Then Catherine's assistant shows a pretty dress to the patient and explains that after her surgery she will be given a new dress. After a few weeks of recovery she will be able to leave the hospital and return to her village. Catherine and her assistant begin to make the sound of drums, as they describe how her village will be surprised to see her return and they will welcome back this restored woman. The woman now has a smile on her face and I have tears on mine.

During the past thirty years the Hamlins and their Ethiopian colleagues have restored more than 7,000 women through this life-changing surgery. In conversations with both Reg and Catherine over the years, they have expressed the joy and continuing satisfaction that accompanies sharing with others. They are adamant that this would never have happened if they hadn't followed their conviction to make fistula pilgrims their mission. Reg Hamlin died a few years ago, but Catherine, now in her seventies, is determined to carry on. She describes this work as a "labour of love."

Generous acts have the unique ability to lift us to a higher level where we are more human, more the person we really want to be. In the very act of encouraging someone else we are graced with awareness that life is better. Generosity has the power to make us feel better about helping others.

Will generosity save our lives? Yes, it can be an essential element in enriching our lives, building a more co-operative future, improving our emotional and physical health and simply making life more fun. It's also a very serious business because our society is showing the strains of violence, poverty, selfishness and neglect. Generosity is the attitude that puts heart in our obligation to care for others. Generosity from those who have is part of the solution. While the number of believers is growing, there is a pressing need to nurture and recruit yet more believers in this powerful way to change our life together. The generosity journey is looking for more travellers.

"It doesn't take a hero to act like a human being. We all have it—the makings of a pretty good person is standard equipment."

(Lewis Smedes)

Chapter Two

Who Are the Generous?

Generous people are everywhere, but their stories are not told often enough. Who are they and where do they come from? Sometimes it's children who give us the most powerful examples.

Recently a mother sent me a note about the unusual compassion her daughter felt for those she described as "the poor people." Five-year-old Madelyn, at her own initiative, prays for them every night. Her simple prayer, "God, don't help us any; just help the poor people," reflects child-like simplicity and a concern that touches her family in a special way. And Madelyn has put her prayer into action by giving her small savings of five dollars to help those in need. In her example there is a deep truth about child-like compassion and daily persistence. Her generosity is both felt and expressed.

Children have an uncanny way of connecting their thoughts with their actions. For them, if you really mean it, you will do something about it. As adults, we sometimes fail to act because we see all the complexities. It's not uncommon for our knowledge to paralyze our expression of compassion.

At times I struggle with this tension in my travels to places of disaster and profound human need. It's overwhelming to see starving children and know that unless the system changes we can't help them all. Yet, time after time, I see examples of adults who drop their normal role or job to relate personally to children. It's not enough to help someone at a distance; there is a persistent desire to do something personal. My experience with film crews in poor countries is one example. On numerous occasions the filming will come to a stop as one of the crew takes a few minutes to play and relate to one of the children we are filming. It's a gentle reminder that even though we can't help every child who suffers, we can be vulnerable and intimately involved with the children we help. Connecting even the deepest of our motivations with a tangible expression brings integrity to what we feel. A simple, generous act frequently cuts right to the heart of the matter.

In 1995, Craig Kielburger was a bright grade seven student who was doing some research for a social studies project. In the course of some reading he was drawn to the plight of a boy in Pakistan who was standing up against child labour practices. Children were being put in jobs to pay off family debts and, in the worst cases, their servitude could extend for a lifetime. The jobs are often dangerous, with work days as long as twelve hours, and the children have no opportunity for even the most basic education. Craig was appalled that something like this should be happening to someone his own age. He began to talk to some of his classmates, and they started a homegrown advocacy movement called "Free the Children." They raised money, invited other schools to join them, and today have a network of more than 100,000 students in thirty-five countries supporting these efforts.

Since then, Craig has travelled to many countries to see the situation first hand. On his first trip to Southeast Asia, where child labour is a daily reality for thousands of children, he managed to arrange a meeting with Canada's Prime Minister, Jean Chrétien, who was also travelling, and challenged him to do more for children trapped in these intolerable conditions. "Free the Children" has raised public concern for child labour to an unprecedented level. They have built more than 350 schools that provide daily education for 20,000 children.[1]

Craig's compassion and motivation reflect a generosity of spirit toward others that reinforces the concern of young people and the way a very basic concern for others can turn into actions that really make a difference. He has not allowed the complexities of the child labour situation to undermine both the responsibility and the capacity to respond. Craig Kielburger and other children like him can be some of our best teachers for a more generous and caring world.

Even children caught in situations of tragedy that defy the human imagination can still practise generosity. Sierra Leone's civil war has been brutal, especially for children. Some of the rebel fighters have practised forced amputation to send a message to the civilian population. Domba, a beautiful eight-year-old girl, faced the terror of having her left hand amputated. Then, while still in shock, she watched the rebels amputate her mother's left hand as well. When I met her, she was living with her mother and other amputees in a camp in the capital city of Freetown.

Domba's dark brown eyes shone with energy, and when I asked what she would like to do in the future she said, "I want to get an education so that I can help my mother." Her immediate response was to pursue a future that would enable her to help someone else. Generous people see the world differently. The focus shifts away from self and personal interest.

Generosity can emerge out of the most horrific experiences. And, in some cases, people are willing to make the ultimate sacrifice and risk their lives to help others.

Samuel Oliner survived the Holocaust as a Jewish boy in Hitler's Europe. A peasant Christian family who passed him off as a Gentile saved his life. Later, after resettlement and a new life in the United States, he researched some of the estimated 50,000 cases of non-Jews who rescued Jewish people from certain death in concentration camps. If there were ever examples of human generosity and bravery, these rescuers offered clues about the motivation and formation of brave, caring behaviour.

Oliner found that education and religion were not determinant factors. Instead, he found that the rescuers had learned generosity from at least one of their parents who modelled generous and caring behaviour for someone *beyond their local group or clan*. Oliner called this "extensivity." It was also important that the parent used reasoning and induction rather than coercive discipline to teach their children to be caring. There was a strong appeal to the child's level of understanding even though she or he might lack experience in the wider adult world.

Another amazing feature to this story is that Oliner himself was healed and transformed by his research on those who had rescued Jewish people. Though he began as an extremely suspicious, intro- verted victim, in the course of his research he saw the hopeful and positive side of human life, and it changed him forever. Colleagues now describe Oliner as an engaging, outgoing, positive individual who is a delightful companion. His past of horror and deprivation has miraculously been transformed by exposure to generous, self-giving behaviour.[2]

There is still a certain mystery around those who practise generosity. Why is it that certain people are generous? On the one hand it is clear that they give because they believe it is right and good. At the same time it is also apparent that they receive some personal satisfaction from giving in this way. Great martyrs of our time such as Mahatma Gandhi and Martin Luther King put their lives on the line for what they believed, but it cannot be denied that they received personal satisfaction in giving of themselves.

Even the example of Jesus experiencing the horrors of the crucifixion shows that he was satisfying what the Bible speaks of as God's redemptive plan for the world. "And going a little farther, he threw himself on the ground and prayed, 'My Father, if it is possible, let this cup pass from me; yet not what I want but what you want.'" (Matthew 26:39, NRSV)

Jesus knowingly sacrificed his own life for others while gaining a personal satisfaction that he was doing the right thing. His satisfaction reflected his desire to submit to the plan of God. It seems right to admit that generous behaviour connects with the personal satisfaction of the giver.

We lead ourselves into a dead end if we separate generosity from some level of personal satisfaction. We might behave compassionately even if it causes us discomfort, but we cannot do something that fails to satisfy us. The choice is ours. It's a reference to our will and the freedom to exercise it. More and more it appears that we were created to find satisfaction in serving others. It is humanly impossible to disconnect our generous actions from a corresponding benefit in doing the right thing. Of course the truly generous will explain that on some occasions generosity requires great effort because they don't feel much satisfaction, but they continue to give.

Perhaps the issue revolves around the attitude taken by the generous person. In the examples I've just given, personal concern was always secondary. The focus was on others and how one could best help. This attitude is the fine line between true generosity and giving to get something in return. Others might argue that attitude is irrelevant and that what really counts is whether a person reaches out to help someone in need. The recipient of such help might be tempted to agree, but I wonder. Most of us can remember an experience when someone has offered help, but his or her real priority was to receive credit or recognition. If we need the help badly enough we will accept it, but given any other option we are likely to refuse it. Generosity is more than giving; it's offering help with the right attitude. This is one of the distinguishing marks of the truly generous person.

E. Stanley Jones, a missionary and Christian leader for more than fifty years, expresses the spirit of the enthusiast: "It's doing everything for fun. And you do everything for nothing. You love God for nothing; you love others for nothing. You serve God for nothing."[3] Jones spoke publicly every day for more than forty years and authored countless books, many of them bestsellers in the 1950s and '60s. It's a reminder that we shouldn't make generosity and serving too complicated. There is a spontaneous quality that should be respected and nurtured.

Philosopher Lewis Smedes also reminds us that we must keep life simple or caring can be undermined. He relates a Friesland folktale of a sad Friesian clerk named Fopke, who is convinced that everyone despises him. As a final desperate act to prove his manhood, he decides to commit suicide by shooting himself. On a cold winter evening he makes his preparations. He is seated at a table with a revolver that contains one bullet. Fopke decides it would be more heroic if he downed one glass of Dutch gin and then shot himself while throwing the empty glass out the window. His head would slump to the table, leaving him in a final posture of dignity.

As Fopke drinks the full glass of gin he falls into a deep sleep and dreams he is in another place. The village is populated by human-like people who are incredibly caring and transparent. They accept him wholeheartedly, inviting him into their homes and sharing their delicious food. Fopke also notices that they never lock their doors at night, no one is rude to others and they are at peace with themselves. He becomes curious and begins to ask them questions. Much to his surprise he discovers that they have never heard of goodness and virtue. They invite Fopke to instruct them in these matters, so he takes a Socratic approach by asking questions about badness. They begin to learn of things such as killing, rape, thievery and conflict. Soon they talk of nothing but goodness and badness.

In response to all this talk of good and evil, a great change comes upon the land. Everyone is afraid of strangers; they no longer keep their homes open or offer food to visitors. They lie to each other to protect themselves. It becomes a time of fear and darkness. Fopke begins to realize what a terrible thing he has introduced to this once innocent and caring people. He pleads with them to go back to their old ways and practise care and generosity toward each other, but they laugh and condemn him. They tell him he is simple-minded and refuse to speak to him.

Fopke awakes from this momentous dream, and he decides to change his life because "it is far, far better to be good than to think about being good." The local villagers realize that something has changed in Fopke; the irritable clerk has become someone who cares for others. Soon they are seeking his opinion on life and he offers his counsel with wisdom and maturity. Eventually they ask Fopke to explain how he became a changed person, a good person. He says, "I cannot talk about it. And please do not call me good. Only God is good. I am only on the Way. Join me if you will, but please do not ask me to speak of it." Fopke continued his commendable life in the village, doing good among his people. When he died, the local Friesian community buried his body in a grave near the sea with these words on a wooden marker: "All things considered, a pretty good person."[4]

What we do will speak louder than words and how we travel on the way is a very personal matter. In his seventies, Don Winsor suffers from a severe heart condition and requires various medications to treat his illness. Yet none of this detracts from his volunteering activities. His passion is to place small counter-top displays in stores and offices that invite customers to donate their change to help hungry children. His "trap line" of displays across the province of Newfoundland numbers over 360. He is a dynamo of enthusiasm. In one recent two-year stretch, he raised $39,000 to feed the world's hungry children. When asked how he manages the many eight-hour days of driving to monitor the displays he says, "The last two years of my life have been the best ever. I wouldn't trade this experience for anything."

Who are the generous? They are ordinary people who do little things and big things to help others. Generosity can truly be the mortar that binds us together as caring members of the human family.

The former prime minister of Australia, Bob Hawke, described a major turning point in his life while attending an international youth convention in India. In an effort to deal with the crowds, organizers had a high fence constructed to keep the local people separated from those attending the convention. At times the Indian children would be begging for food from those on the other side of the fence. Hawke found this separation hypocritical, especially when the leaders and missionaries organizing the event were supposed to be there to help others. He sensed an attitude toward the local people that was condescending and patronizing. All the good works seemed compromised by self-righteousness and insensitivity. It was an agonizing experience and it contributed to Hawke's determination to always fight for the underdog.

Sometimes it's when we encounter injustices and

brutal behaviour that we're reminded how important generosity and fairness really are. I visited Tuol Sleng prison in Cambodia for the first time in 1982. At one time it was a school, but the Khmer Rouge turned it into an execution chamber for those they considered traitors after they invaded the city of Phnom Penh in 1974. Their philosophy was an insidious one. If there was any hint of a disloyal person in a family or village, everyone would be killed. If you were educated, a businessperson, a teacher, wore glasses or had a political past, you were guaranteed death. The Khmer Rouge's reign of terror took the lives of an estimated one million Cambodians. The Khmer Rouge documented some of their killings with still photographs to prove that the guilty had been exterminated.

Inside Tuol Sleng prison, there is a photograph that embraces all the world's brokenness in one click of the shutter. It is a large black and white photograph, taken in a room where killers operated with impunity. In this photo, a young woman looks straight into the camera lens with fear, apprehension and terror plainly visible in her face. Her large eyes are brimming with tears and one tear spills down her left cheek. As your eye follows the tear downward, you see that she is holding a baby. We do not know their names. We only know that she is in the hands of lunatics who will take her life and the life of her baby. This photo is only one among hundreds that mark the five years of insanity in a small nation of seven million people.

My mind is drawn to those who took this picture. Was there not one ounce of human caring and generosity left? Even if one embraced the Khmer Rouge's brutal political philosophy, would not a decent heart be touched by a young mother with a beautiful baby? It is this image, and so many others like it, that drives every caring person to say "never again" in a world that does it over and over again. The generous person cannot give up or we leave this world to the lunatics who kill our children and extinguish the lights that draw us together.

Who are the generous? They are ordinary people who are driven by an extraordinary desire and attitude to help others. They can be children, teenagers, adults and senior citizens. They cross every religious and cultural boundary. Some work in environments that are more favourable toward generosity, but even in the worst places the spark to care for others shines brightly. The call to be generous is an investment that pays dividends to those who step out in faith. No one need despair that generosity is reserved only for those who have a good education or a special personality. Generosity is for everyone. All it takes is a willing spirit and the courage to be used for something greater than ourselves.

"We are rich only through what we give, and poor only through what we refuse."

(Anne Swetchine)

Chapter Three

The Power of Generosity to Overcome Obstacles

Finding hope and meaning in a world that can be quickly shattered is a daunting task. In the immediate aftermath of a tragedy, there are always people who will respond quickly and generously. Our society places great importance on the need for such a response, and we often give special recognition— quite rightly—to those who go beyond the call of duty in a time of crisis.

My cousin Jonathan has faced many challenges in his life. Adopted by my aunt and uncle at infancy, he was raised in an environment of affection and care.

Despite his loving upbringing, Jonathan was lured into reckless behaviour that ultimately came with a heavy price. A troubled marriage to an addicted partner produced three boys in quick succession. The marriage fell apart and Jonathan took sole custody of the boys.

Jonathan's commitment to fatherhood and parenting in the midst of his own personal trials has been an act of tremendous courage. In spite of physical challenges, unemployment and all the pressures that sometimes lead men to abandon their responsibilities as fathers, Jonathan has stood his ground. Of course, it hasn't been easy, even with faithful support from his parents. Not long ago, however, this struggling family encountered another crisis, which had the potential to end in tragedy.

Jonathan's youngest son, six-year-old Joey, was experiencing occasional fainting spells that appeared to be epileptic in nature. One day, after accepting a perfect attendance award in a school assembly, Joey returned to his seat, suddenly fainted and stopped breathing. He was turning blue as a doctor and a pastor who were at the assembly raced to his side. The doctor began giving CPR, while the pastor knelt at Joey's feet pleading before God to save this boy's life. Seven minutes passed, until finally Joey regained consciousness. Later examination established that without the doctor's aggressive and persistent use of CPR Joey would have died.

Here were two strangers willing to react instantly on behalf of someone they did not know. I expect they never thought twice about responding. A little boy was going to die; they responded. They were not obliged to act, but they did. This response is another example of generosity in action—an attitude combined with skill and experience that brings change. In that moment, grace and generosity locked together in an act of caring. The generous spirit of two people willing to act in the midst of a crisis ultimately saved the life of a little boy.

Joey was later diagnosed with long QT syndrome, a condition that causes the heart to stop beating. A defibrillator was subsequently attached to Joey's heart, and though he has to avoid strenuous exercise, he is a healthy boy today.

The image of the two rescuers administering physical and spiritual help demonstrates another aspect of generosity—you can't give what you don't have. The doctor was the expert in administering CPR and the minister was the professional trained for spiritual assistance. They both gave from what they were trained to do. Generosity on many occasions will draw from our training or profession.

Sometimes obstacles in our lives begin with a crisis, but turn into challenges that require great endurance. Paul Baetz, a young man in his midtwenties, had everything going for him when his life took a sudden turn. He was a university graduate with strong family support. His father was a successful executive and his stepmother was an experienced psychiatric nurse. He was athletic and had recently been playing in a semi-pro football league.

Paul joined our church and was very active working with young people. At our annual church picnic he was enjoying a game of pick-up football when, during a routine pass, he felt his knee wrench. During his semi-pro games, he had absorbed some very hard contact causing both his back and knee to be injured, so it was a feeling he recognized. This time, it felt worse.

Over the next few days Paul reluctantly came to the conclusion that he needed knee surgery. In his mind it would be a routine operation that would require therapy, but in the end he would be back playing recreational football before too long. His parents supported his decision and they were there for him as preparations were made for the surgery.

The surgery to the knee was very successful, but as a result of the operation Paul contracted encephalomyelitis, a powerful viral infection that attacks various brain functions. For a few weeks Paul was close to death. He was physically impaired with paralysis in one leg and one arm, but even more importantly his thought processes and speech were deeply affected. At certain points there was concern that he might never recover.

Paul refused to give up, even after being released and then suffering the return of the infection. Months of demanding therapy challenged his patience and perseverance. His religious faith and his immediate family sustained him in the most difficult times. He was also motivated by his desire to get back some semblance of his former life.

Paul decided that he wanted to pursue theological studies. Though he was able to function reasonably well at a physical level, Paul still faced severe limitations in his ability to speak. Paul enrolled in a three-year theological degree program that included heavy academic courses as well as preaching. He described the preaching course as terrifying. Five years later he graduated not to a traditional church ministry, but as a staff member at a drop-in retreat centre called Sanctuary in downtown Toronto.

Paul's desire is to give something back as well as fulfill his deep aspiration to serve others as part of a community. Paul would be the first to say that a major part of his healing is his focus on the needs of others. A generosity of spirit infuses his conversation when he describes his relationships with those who live at the very edge of society. This generosity of spirit not only saved his life, but now contributes to the lives of others as well.

Reflecting on his own situation, Paul described to me the distinction between pity and compassion. People who pity him are a dime a dozen, he says, but those who have genuine compassion are fewer. In his words, compassion is a desire for relationship with the one who is suffering; pity is merely a feeling that, in many cases, avoids relationships. Compassion involves looking toward the other person with generosity and genuine concern; pity involves only our own feelings. Unfortunately, the person who is pitied is often seen as weak and dependent.

As Paul speaks in his measured, thoughtful way, with an occasional gap or stumble, I am struck by how his generosity of spirit is a reflection of deep commitment to God's love and Paul's determination to be generous and caring toward others. Paul's generosity is not only a reflection of who he is, but is also a virtue that is giving life, vitality and meaning to his daily challenges.

Wherever I go in the world, I run headlong into this kind of generosity. In Zambia in southern Africa, Judy Chileshe lives out her generosity in an unassuming yet extraordinary way. Life didn't start out well for her. While she was young, her father divorced her mother and then remarried. From that point on, Judy's life became a nightmare. Her stepmother did everything possible to destroy Judy's relationship with her family. Things deteriorated so badly that her father was forced to intervene and provide a separate house for Judy, her brother and sister.

Judy describes how awkward it was to schedule visits in order to maintain contact with her father. Her stepmother's interference escalated to the point where she even destroyed Judy's schoolbooks. This was particularly devastating because school was where Judy, an intelligent and capable student, found her identity. Judy's teachers assured her she had a future, and could even go on to university. In her native Zambia, securing a university placement is extremely difficult, especially for a girl.

Without schoolbooks, Judy could not study for exams. Her marks declined: from the top of her class, she fell to marginally passing. Her self-esteem and confidence began to diminish. Her life was spiralling downward. Hope soon withered to the point of despair.

In re-telling this, Judy becomes thoughtful and reflective. "My teachers saved my life," she says. They observed her depression and failing performance, took her aside, and gave her special tutoring. They encouraged her not to give up. They would find a way for her to get to school. Her religious life reawakened at this point as well. Judy's grades began a dramatic improvement and she scored highly on the competitive graduates exam. Judy was accepted to a university, where she chose a nursing course. After two years she was restless to give something back to her community. With the HIV/AIDS crisis devastating her country, Judy began to search for ways she could be involved and earn even a small salary.

The AIDS crisis has affected Zambia so profoundly that an estimated 21 percent of the adult population is HIV-positive. Major sources of infection are the transport routes that go north and south through sub-Saharan Africa. Truck drivers, away from home for extended periods, patronize the prostitutes at stops along the way. Some of the most infected areas are the borders between countries where drivers often wait for more than a day to pass inspection. The environment provides a context for dangerous and irresponsible sexual behaviour.

The women serving as sex workers are often from poor families, desperate to put bread on the table. Increasingly, however, they become the victims in the deadly HIV/AIDS crisis. It begins when husbands and fathers die from the virus, leaving the women as the surviving breadwinners for the family. Prostitution is the only alternative for many young women. Some are single parents with children at home who would go hungry unless they plied the trade. In some cases, teenage girls whose mothers are sick become the only support for their siblings. It becomes a choice between letting your family go hungry or accepting money for sex.

Judy saw this new reality emerging in her home city of Livingstone on the border of Zambia and Zimbabwe. Here was a chance to be part of a program that was alerting truck drivers and prostitutes to the dangers of their lifestyle, and offering medical care and counselling. This in-your-face community work would be a challenge, but Judy felt a calling. In her worst moments as a teenager, she recalled how close she was to giving up. A life of prostitution would have been right around the corner for her, if her teachers had not intervened.

Judy describes to me the passion she feels for this work. She tells me, "This is not a job, this is a calling. I have to do this." In her deliberate way, she tells the story of her older sister who was so overwhelmed by the abuse of their early years that she escaped into a marriage at an early age. Tragically the man

she married was HIV-positive, so she became infected as well. Not long after giving birth to a little
girl, Judy's sister died of full-blown AIDS. Judy
now cares for her three-year-old niece.

Generosity goes deep in Judy's life. She recounts
how she regularly visits her father and stepmother
who are experiencing difficulties. None of her
other family members are prepared to offer any
help, but Judy goes faithfully. "They are still my parents," she says, with a light in her eye. And, after
years of separation, she has managed to re-unite
with her birth mother as well.

People like Judy give profound hope that the
HIV/AIDS crisis can be overcome in Zambia. Yet it
will not happen without help from the larger
world. Judy and other African brothers and sisters
are giving every ounce of commitment to bring
hope. Their message of ABC—Abstain from sex if
you are not married, Be faithful if you are married
and if you fail use a Condom—is part of the most
effective response to this crisis. Church members
and other volunteers are trained to counsel and support those who are infected. Donations from overseas governments, the World Bank and private
individuals are increasing, but there is still less than
one-third of the required fifteen billion dollars
committed to battle this epidemic. People like Judy

Chileshe are hoping and praying that we will respond.

Generosity, combined with deep compassion, is making changes in our world. The obstacles that life brings can be turned into opportunities. Hard, practical and gritty decision-making, followed by practical action, is an inspiration for anyone on the generosity journey. Much can be accomplished, but there is much to do.

"The world of the generous gets larger and larger;
the world of the stingy gets smaller and smaller."
(Proverbs 11:24, The Message translation)

Chapter Four

The Power of Generosity to Stimulate Personal Growth

Generosity is about people, and it starts with you and me. If we are going to grow, it will be in relationship with someone else, however brief or fleeting. We have to pursue opportunities to express our care and concern for others. Our commitment to grow will require risk-taking and a willingness to move outside of our comfort zones. The journey will take us into situations that challenge our culture's high value on self-interest.

I was at a check-out counter at the local supermarket and I noticed a boy about ten standing next to the woman who was operating the cash register. He had a tag on his shirt indicating that he was helping his mother. As she passed the items across the scanner he packed them in the shopping bag. It was a great moment because of his transparent satisfaction in helping his mother. There was a smile on his face that was matched by her look of affection.

In the midst of my shopping, I was taken by this little episode. Without thinking much, I reached into my pocket and fished out a dollar coin. Catching the lad's attention I leaned toward him and said, "Any young man who helps his mother like you are doing deserves something special. Here's a loonie—have a soda pop on me at your next break." He hesitated for a moment, looked up at his mother and then accepted the coin. This whole episode took about two minutes.

Generosity begins with someone taking a risk, making a gesture. It starts with one person. Yet it's far more complicated than simply what I choose to do. The recipient is part of the exchange as well. This boy took my gesture well. He was encouraged and in fact gave me a big smile. His mother did too. But it wasn't over.

Seconds later, the woman behind me in line said, "What did you do that for? Now he'll expect something from all of us!" My balloon was deflated, and my first reaction was to snap back at her small-mindedness. Fortunately, I maintained control of myself and simply let the situation pass. In fact, the woman's comment was a judgment on her. Only later did I realize that generosity has not only an initiating person and a respondent, but also a secondary public that observes and in some way participates.

Yet even this small episode underscores again the centrality of the person who initiates the act of generosity. What causes us to want to reach out to someone else? Perhaps I was looking for a feel-good moment, yet there was a moral edge to my thinking. I believe we have to make a choice between people being encouraged in their lives or being discouraged. And that matters for both spiritual and moral reasons to me. The idea that everyone should be left alone to hope for the best is grossly inadequate. I have experienced the personal joy and uplift when someone goes out of his or her way to be generous and caring. If I am generous to someone, that person will likely be generous to someone else. There is an argument to be made that the universe was created to operate this way. In past years there has been talk of the phenomenon called "random acts of kindness." The movie *Pay It Forward* dramatizes the idea by showing a boy who gives his life to this idea of caring for others. Generosity starts with someone taking the initiative.

Generosity doesn't come easily. Time and again we're inspired by stories of generous people who have really made a difference, yet it is not enough to get us to take action. Even if caring gives us a good feeling, we still need to take the initiative and reach out to someone in a specific situation. Professor Ed Bennet of Wilfrid Laurier University made the following comment after completing his research on the pursuit of happiness, "Our society is promoting a form of self-centred and egocentric behaviour that is counter-productive to the wellness and happiness of people and communities."[1] In our North American culture, generosity is under threat. We are increasingly becoming the "me first" society with no brakes on the accelerator that drives our greed and consumption. The attack on generosity is driven by the two things that we value most: time and money. One drives the other. If you have time you will be always pressed to use it primarily to work, so you can acquire the toys and trappings that our culture values. But after accomplishing that, many people find their time is in too short a supply to allow them to enjoy the very things that really matter. Time and money both conspire to hold us back from sharing and giving in important ways, whether it's time with our families or volunteer work for important causes. The attack on generosity also undermines our willingness to give financially to causes that address the social issues of our time. We have to make choices to give up some of our time and money to nurture the compassion and generosity that hold us together as families, communities, nations and the world.

At some point we have to take the chance to demonstrate acts of caring and sharing. We can't wait until we are certain that everything is right. Personal growth through generosity won't happen unless we are prepared to go places that may make us feel uncomfortable. Some people are very sensitive to what others might think, and will find it too risky to offer a gesture that can be refused, ignored or misinterpreted. Some people are shy by nature, others find it difficult to read relational situations quickly, while still others see the glass half empty rather than half full. These and any number of personality traits can affect our ability to reach out in acts of generosity. These are all reasons that make generosity a little harder, but they only become excuses when we refuse to overcome them.

In our office we have an incredible person named Lori West. She suffers from a degenerative disease called familial spastic dysplegia. It's a rare illness, found in one out of every ten million adults, and it affects the nervous system and the muscles. There is no effective treatment. Lori, who was once a competitive public speaker, can hardly speak. In fact she legally changed her name from Donna West to Lori West because it was so difficult to say the letter "d." Lori was determined to say her own name as long as she could. Now it's very difficult to understand her speech at all, so Lori uses a talking computer that produces synthesized speech. The physical effects of the disease have created other problems as well. It's very difficult for her to walk. She was forced to have three toes removed so she can still wear shoes. Now she is mostly confined to a wheelchair.

All of this happened to her after growing up in a very dysfunctional home where she was subjected to both physical and emotional abuse. On one occasion her mother attacked her with the intention of taking her life.

In the midst of all these difficulties, Lori is a generous person because she has made a decision to grow. She won't let her unique challenges diminish her opportunity to care for others. Her passion is writing short stories and poetry. She is fully engaged in life, and her generosity overflows in her concern for others. In our office Lori writes and edits our staff publication as well as tracks and distributes all the requests for prayer from the problem situations around the world. Her monthly editorials display a mature Christian faith that looks at the world with eyes wide open and a heart full of compassion.

I can think of few people with more reason to rage at life than Lori. Yet she chooses to see the good, the beautiful and the courageous, the triumphs in the midst of the tragedies. Somehow, with the grace of God, she approaches each situation with generosity and goodwill. It would be easier for Lori to feel sorry for herself, but she makes a choice every day to see light and joy rather than sorrow and despair.

We often learn generosity by example and our parents can be powerful teachers. When I was a boy living on a dairy farm, I became upset with my mother over some mishap that, to my seven-year-old mind, seemed grave indeed. In a fit of pique, I announced that I was running away. With her usual wisdom and cleverness, Mom responded by saying that if I were running away I would need some food and water. She carefully made me a peanut butter sandwich and presented me with a Mason jar full of water. Out the door I went, and down the road for about a mile.

As my footsteps carried me away, I became less and less confident that this was a good idea. Finally I stopped, ate the sandwich, opened the jar, drank some water and then poured the rest out on the road. Walking back, I considered how I was going to avoid the obvious embarrassment over my bad decision. As I marched into the farm kitchen trying to be both nonchalant and humble, I announced to my mother that I had returned. When she asked me why, I spoke confidently that I had run out of water. With a true generosity of spirit, she didn't pursue it any further. I escaped with my dignity, yet was thoroughly self-chastised about the foolishness of my action. To this day, when my Type-A personality is tempted to jump in with long justifications or questionings with staff or family, I think of my mother and the empty water jar defense. Keeping quiet and letting someone navigate their own mistakes is an important insight. My mother thought twice before reacting to my behaviour, and in the end she let me work it out for myself. Rather than berate me for my obvious foolishness, Mom had confidence in my ability to grow from this experience. That small gesture of generosity from my mother has stimulated more growth than I ever imagined.

Personal growth can be a selfish pursuit if we hold it too tightly. Our growing happens when we give up more than we hold on to. Generosity becomes one of those attitudes and actions that open us to new possibilities. I like to describe this reality as the reciprocity cycle. We don't give because we get, but we do get after the fact. In most situations, generosity reaps its own reward. The satisfaction provides an invaluable, uplifting experience. People who practise generosity over a lifetime develop an internal "wiring" that helps them see possibilities more often than barriers. Generosity, when regularly practised, produces a kind of emotional DNA that can be passed on to our children. Our practice becomes a model for them.

But opting for generosity doesn't necessarily mean it will be easy. I'm amazed at my own journey. Sometimes I think I do pretty well. Then on other occasions I slip back into behaviour that denies who I really want to be.

I was in Africa in the city of Luanda, Angola, paying a visit to the Canadian consular office there. At the entrance I was met by a well-dressed Angolan security guard who took my passport and then requested that I open every compartment of my case. I was already late and had just come from the American embassy, where my bag hadn't been searched at all. In an embarrassingly ungenerous way, I let my actions and gestures communicate my irritation with this procedure. Eventually I passed the test and made it to the scheduled appointment.

At the conclusion of my meeting, I passed back outside and retrieved my passport. As the guard gave me the passport, he said to me, "There is no difficulty. I am not the problem." It was his way of telling me that he was simply following the procedures that had been outlined for him. He was a professional doing his job. I shook his hand, thanked him and then went on my way.

Then suddenly I felt that I should do more. All I had with me was a Canada pin, so I walked back and gave it to him and expressed my apology. We shook hands. I felt that we had connected and something that was patently ungenerous had been in some way redressed.

Growth requires getting out of our comfort zone and generosity is no different. If it came easily, we would see much more of it. One of the most dramatic expressions of generosity I know of occurred with one of my good friends, Don Cousens, the mayor of Markham, Ontario. Don's family from his father's side carries the genetic code for a disease called polycystic kidney disease. Both Don's father and older brother died of the disease. Now, at age sixty-four, Don was facing the strong likelihood of death unless he received a new kidney. The average waiting period in Canada is three years unless you receive a kidney from a live donor. Don's wife,

Aline, was not a match, so the picture was bleak.

Word got out to Don Clayton, who has been a good friend of Don Cousens for more than twenty years. Even at sixty-two, Clayton couldn't imagine life without his good friend. Twenty different acquaintances would eventually offer a kidney, but it was Don Clayton who offered first, and subsequent testing confirmed that he was the best match. After removal of one of his bad kidneys, Don Cousens began the procedure to receive a new one and Don Clayton began the process to give one up. The operation was a complete success.

In a recent newspaper interview, Don Clayton commented, "Now he is the brother I never had. We're connected forever and I genuinely like that." Clayton is just as straightforward when describing why he did it, "I did it because I happen to like—no, love—Don. I can't imagine seeing that man die without me doing something to help him. It's what friendship is all about."[2] Today Don Cousens enjoys better health than he has for years, and Don Clayton has fully recovered as well.

Generosity often operates at the most everyday level of experience. Walking down the street can become a moral dilemma as panhandlers on the street can present a great challenge to those wishing to be generous. Do I give or not? If I give, how will my money be used? If the person has a substance addiction, will I be contributing to this destructive habit? In our increasingly de-personalized society, in which family breakdown is common, more people are living on the streets. Diminishing public support for institutionalized care means that more people with significant mental and emotional health problems are left to their own devices. The safety net is shrinking and, for so many, panhandling has become a way of life.

What is our responsibility? Panhandlers deserve to be treated as human beings. They are ignored and even abused by the passersby they face everyday. Whether we choose to give money or not, our first obligation in a caring society is to acknowledge their presence. Looking away is a form of denial that diminishes and distances at the same time. Generosity sets a standard that builds relationships rather than destroys them.

One of the great measures of a person's generosity is how he or she relates to people at different levels in an organization. Almost every staff member observes how a senior person relates to others. Generosity happens when we step outside our position to do the thing that reflects our person and not our level of authority. Healthy, balanced leaders make sure they join activities where they are followers, not necessarily the person in charge. Ordinary work and routine chores give us perspective and humility.

The most successful managers in a recent study by the Centre for Creative Leadership are those who score the highest on affection—both expressed and wanted. These managers show warmth and fondness toward those who work for them while wanting the same for themselves. The researchers state, "They get closer to people, and they're significantly more open in sharing their thoughts and feelings than their lower-performing counterparts . . . the best leaders want to be liked, and they want openness from other people."[3] To reinforce their point, the researchers explain that the affection characteristic is the only factor to significantly differentiate the top quartile of managers from the bottom quartile.

This research should come as no surprise. As far back as 1949, Lawrence Lindahl conducted a study that asked employees and managers to "rank the intangible rewards of their jobs." Both groups rated "feeling appreciated" the highest. The study was repeated in the 1980s and 1990s and the results were the same.[4] Employees and managers want the same thing—to be appreciated.

One aspect of Mahatma Gandhi's philosophy of

life was his conviction that everyone should take responsibility for the chores of daily living. His regular time at the spinning wheel producing his own fabric was a message to an entire country. Missionary E. Stanley Jones developed a retreat centre following Gandhi's example. Every participant spent time mopping floors and cleaning toilets. These tasks remind us that all kinds of work are important and to be valued. Regardless of where we are in the work hierarchy, work well done has significance. The value of work rests not in the level of the worker, but in the competency with which it is completed. Generosity has a similar quality. It's not what position you have, but rather what position are you prepared to put yourself in, in order to serve others.

"When a person is down in the world, an ounce of help is better than a pound of preaching."

(Edward G. Bulwer-Lytton)

"Fertilizer does no good in a heap, but a little spread around works miracles all over."

(Percy Ross)

Chapter Five

The Power of Generosity: Does It Make a Difference?

Talking about ideas brings its own rewards, but at some point we have to ask—do these ideas actually work? Does the theory connect with reality? Generosity is no exception. It must be more than a good feeling. Somehow it must help us connect with the grit and grime of everyday living. Does it make life better? Is generosity a do-gooder's delusionary proposal to a world that knows better? Is it realistic to think that significant numbers of people will actually embrace generosity in new and greater ways?

Little children often provide examples of how generosity can make a difference. They expand the numbers of those who care and their consciences are easily stirred. Recently, I received a letter from a mother describing her daughter's determination to help children overseas. Six-year-old Heather had seen the needs of hungry children in Africa through a television program. The awareness would not leave her. Her thoughts were basic: these children need help; they must be afraid; what am I going to do?

So Heather put her feelings into action and through various projects she raised $206. Her mother sent the money to World Vision along with a note that described Heather's concern for children who didn't have parents. She had seen pictures of children living on their own because war or HIV/AIDS had taken the lives of their parents. Heather was relieved that her gift would help children who lived at the very edge of life. Her parents had encouraged her to be generous, and together they created a memory that will last Heather a lifetime.

Generosity can emerge as a broad public response as well as an individual one. The terrorist attacks against the United States on September 11, 2001, provoked more than anger and the desire for revenge. Tens of thousands rose to the challenge by giving in extraordinary ways. Many travelled to the disaster site and offered to search for the missing. Others counselled and offered encouragement. At St. Paul's Chapel, which was adjacent to the crash site yet miraculously untouched by the devastating attack, volunteers and church staff created an oasis of comfort and rehabilitation for the emergency workers. They offered food, drink, counselling, body massage and prayer. The walls and ceilings were covered with inscriptions and drawings that renewed and encouraged the tired bodies and despairing spirits. The healing environment was palpable to even the casual visitor. One of the emerging sentiments was generosity—tender gifts to those who were recovering bodies and nurturing the lingering hope that someone might still be rescued.

After 9/11 there was an overwhelming response from the American public to volunteer their time and offer financial assistance. People donated more than one billion dollars to various private charities.[1] Thousands upon thousands seized the opportunity to be generous toward those who faced personal loss. Perhaps even more significantly, many people were challenged at the most fundamental level regarding what's important in life. A teary-eyed fireman described how, prior to 9/11, he was preparing for divorce over differences with his spouse. It would break up their family, including two children. After 9/11 he concluded that nothing was more important than family relationships and he expressed a determination to make his marriage work.

Canadians identified with the victims and their families as well. Volunteers crossed the border to help. They made donations, offered expertise and said prayers. Out of this tragedy may emerge long-term positive influences that encourage generosity and care for others that weren't there prior to 9/11. A generosity of spirit can be found in the midst of national mourning and loss.

Canada's record of private generosity during the Afghanistan intervention is particularly interesting. Aid agencies raised millions of dollars from the public to offer relief and aid to those suffering in Afghanistan. This response confirmed that Canadians were making an important distinction between the former government of Afghanistan and the pressing needs of the civilian population.

I am convinced that women and men can practise generosity in new ways if they are invited to be part of something larger than themselves. On a trip to the West African country of Mauritania with singer Tom Cochrane, we journeyed to a regional capital called Kiffa to see World Vision's work. It is a dry, dusty, ramshackle, desert town surrounded by sand dunes. The temperature was 40 degrees Celsius. Two large, billowing pieces of fabric had been mounted on poles to offer shade in the desiccating heat. A few hundred people had gathered, women on one side and men on the other, to acknowledge our presence and to comment on the work being done. These people were some of the poorest in the town. Life is hard in Kiffa—there is high infant mortality, few social services of any kind and very limited awareness of how to tackle the obstacles to development.

Mauritania is an official Islamic republic, so the gender roles are different from ours in the West. I was surprised that the first speaker after our greeting was a woman. Her voice was strong as she described how, prior to World Vision's community development work, the people in the community had not worked together. They were not caring properly for their children and too many died of illness. But then she said, "Now things are different. We have learned to work together. We have learned that we can bring change. Our children are in school and they are much healthier. Thank you, World Vision, for helping us."

The crowd applauded and soon more men and women wanted to speak. It was an incredible experience to hear the story of a journey toward dignity, self-reliance and hope. Generosity had played a significant role. Canadians, by sponsoring Kiffa's children, had given generously so that the community development work could begin. And then the Mauritanians from this poor community seized the opportunity to take a risk, share their lives and try a new way to live together. It was a potent blend of community interest supported by self-interest. If they worked together they could see advantages individually and for each other. Generosity helped open the door just a little bit, so that a first step could be taken. The positive results enabled the entire community to embrace new possibilities and move forward together. Now an entire community is experiencing generosity and cooperation in a new and powerful way. More travellers have joined the generosity journey.

Increasing the number of generous people is a good thing, but is it actually making a difference? Is life better? In Kiffa, Mauritania, they would show you healthier children, clean water, more schools and the common pursuit of working together as tangible signs of generosity that makes a difference.

On the other side of Africa in Tanzania, I met

Susannah Nhwagi, who is an AIDS counsellor. Nominated for this position by her community, Susannah does this work as a volunteer. In a community where the likely infection rate is more than 20 percent, only three people have been identified as HIV-positive. There are certainly more, but the stigma attached to AIDS discourages people from having a test done to determine their status. Susannah visits her three clients regularly, offering advice on how to cope with HIV/AIDS, suggestions for an improved diet, and instructions on proper hygiene and lifestyle to prevent infecting others. Most important, she tells me that she shares stories of hope to encourage those who are suffering. If they wish, she will pray with them.

Susannah introduced me to twenty-year-old Esther, a very slender young woman who is HIV-positive. Esther described Susannah's help as a lifeline. She explained how much she likes to talk with Susannah. The hardest time was when Esther was hospitalized, and they struggled to overcome the ensuing despair. Susannah says it was only their faith in God that got them through.

What is often hardest for Esther is the isolation that she faces on a daily basis. Though some people are caring, many others stay away because they are afraid of becoming infected. Susannah explains that one of her chief tasks is to help Esther remember the good times in her life.

Susannah's willingness to share her precious time is a great gift. She is a mother with four children and a husband and yet she gives her time generously. Not only does she counsel the afflicted, she is also a key educator in the community to inform everyone about how HIV/AIDS is spread, how to protect themselves and how to care for those who are infected. She practises generosity that makes a difference.

For generosity to truly work, it needs to benefit both the giver and receiver. Often for the giver it is more intangible. It's the satisfaction that your gift, your gesture, has made a difference. In many situations that is enough. For those who receive generosity, the gift must be of some use, whether practical or emotional. Otherwise generosity has little value.

Generosity is also seen as a characteristic of good businesses. It makes a difference in how a business is evaluated and known. A recent survey and report by Walker Information shows that businesses with a record of generosity to charities are more attractive to their major stakeholders. Corporate generosity is one of the major factors used to differentiate one company from another. Employees admire a company that does good deeds. In fact, as many as one-third or more of a company's employees see a good giving record as a major reason to remain with the company.

One-third of a company's shareholders say that corporate generosity affects the bottom line, has a positive impact on stock performance and influences their decision as to where to invest. Finally, one out of every three customers says a company's giving record would be a reason to choose its products or services. [2]

Generosity also has an influence on the way we conduct business. Good business manners encourage us to accept the cup of tea or coffee offered at the beginning of a business meeting. First, it's good etiquette to accept something that is offered freely. The gesture establishes a positive environment for doing business. Offering a beverage hearkens back to a time when travelling was far more physically demanding and good manners demanded that you provide a cup of water to a weary traveller.

Second, there is anecdotal evidence that you are more likely to be successful in achieving your objective if you accept the offer of hospitality. It shows your willingness to be of service, to move beyond your own boundaries and meet the other person's request. Is it a reason to be generous? Perhaps. But more than anything it reveals again how generosity is part of the lubrication that makes life go better by lifting our spirits and reinforcing our connection with someone else.

Generosity makes a profound difference in the life of an individual. I was in meetings recently to create a vision statement for our international organization. As part of a committee with members from various parts of the world, there were numerous times when the scale of our task appeared overwhelming, yet time and again a personal remark or experience would be shared at just the right time. James Tumbuan, World Vision's national director for Indonesia, reminded us that thirty-five years ago he was a sponsored child whose only hope rested on the generosity of others. His mother sent him away to an orphanage so he could receive an education. At that time it was her only choice, since she was a single mother with little means of support. James finished high school and then received a university scholarship provided by his sponsor. During our meetings, James commented, "Do you understand that I was a little boy of poverty years ago and now today I am sitting at this table and joining with you to set the future course for the very organization that saved my life?" James currently oversees 500 staff and 60,000 sponsored children.

For James, generosity made a difference, as it has

in the lives of so many individuals. Community development work overseas, businesses that give generously and countries that respond to national tragedies all demonstrate the power of caring for others. The opportunity to reach out to someone is an opportunity to bring positive change. Our dreams for a better future are connected to acts of kindness that serve as shining lights in every corner of the world. Actions great and small will make this dream a reality. Hidden away in each of us is the desire to care for others and the corresponding hope that others will treat us the same way.

Mother Teresa tells a wonderful story about a newly married couple who came to the Missionaries of Charity house in Mumbai, India, and gave her a large amount of money.

I asked them, "Where did you get so much money?" They answered, "We got married two days ago. Before we got married we had decided not to celebrate the wedding, not to buy wedding clothes, not to have a reception or a honeymoon. We wanted to give you the money we saved."

I know what such a decision meant, especially for a Hindu family. That is why I asked them, "But how did you think of such a thing?"

"We love each other so much," they answered, "that we wanted to share the joy of our love with those you serve."

To share—what a beautiful thing![3]

Caring for others makes a powerful difference in the lives of those who choose to give. The generous attitude of this young couple reminds us that no one is too poor to give and no one is too rich to receive.

Gary Williams was a classmate during my high school years. He was an unusual character for a small rural high school and his struggles with his sexuality made him the butt of jokes and occasional mistreatment by others, especially boys. After high school he left town and eventually made his way to Los Angeles. It was a place where his alternative lifestyle was more acceptable, and in his inimitable fashion he made an impact on his surroundings. Gary claimed relationships with celebrities and producers in Hollywood. As a graduate student in Pasadena, I sought Gary out to renew our acquaintance. Our times together were few, but always memorable, for he was still unpredictable, and always full of life. At my wedding, Gary sent us two lovely hand-painted clay doves. They were expensive, a bit kitschy and all Gary. I could imagine the smile on his face when he selected them. Other than brief phone calls, that was my last face-to-face contact with Gary.

Years later, after Gary had moved to New York City, I received the tragic news from my family that Gary had been murdered. The case has never been solved. His agonized, difficult life came to a terrible conclusion. Both doves remain perched on our living room shelf. I recall Gary's gift. A simple piece of art-work reminds me of his spirit and his life. Generosity leaves a legacy in this gentle reminder. I say a quiet prayer, and vow in some corner of my heart to make room for the outsider, the person who is different—all in the important task of redeeming my own life as well as the lives of others. It is not enough, but it is something.

"But let justice roll down like waters, and
righteousness like an ever-flowing stream."

(Amos 5:24, NRSV)

"Charity and justice are worth a thousand ounces
of gold."

(Chinese Proverb)

Chapter Six

The Power of Generosity on the Road to Justice

On the road to justice, generosity might be viewed as a cop-out. It's easier to be a little generous than it is to work for justice. Standing for what is right requires principled responses that refuse to bend when the forces of compromise rise up. Yet the complexity of this issue cannot be denied. From the sale of diamonds that are mined and sold by groups committed to war, to the abusive treatment of girls and women in many countries, the plea for justice is unremitting and critical to our common future. In these challenging situations, people who are generous are part of the solution.

John Perkins was an African American growing up in Mississippi after the Second World War. His older brother Clyde, who had returned home from the war as a decorated soldier, was shot and killed by a local sheriff in a racially motivated incident. It happened outside the small town's movie theatre; Clyde had been refused entrance to the theatre because of racial prejudice. The family decided to send John to California to live with members of the extended family where he would have greater opportunities and, more importantly, escape the racist environment of Mississippi.

John made a new life for himself, graduating from high school, marrying, and then working at a large steel mill. Eventually he became a senior union officer with the respect of his colleagues and a secure lifestyle. During this time he was drawn to examine his religious beliefs. Much to his surprise, he began to attend a church where his children were going to Sunday school. He experienced a profound religious conversion, largely motivated by what John describes as "a profound sense of God's love for me." And even more surprising, John found himself in an all-white church. It was a surprising contrast to the events of his earlier life in Mississippi.

As months and then years passed by, John was increasingly drawn by a powerful spiritual conviction to return to Mississippi and begin work among the community he had left. After a period of family discussion and debate, he and his wife and children packed up and moved back to Mississippi. They began by doing church work, but then John and his wife, Vera Mae, noticed the lack of education, health services and job opportunities in the African American community. They responded by organizing community efforts to address these issues, and raised support from church friends in California to help build a new future. They also organized voter registration drives. It was at the height of the civil rights movement and John's activities were noticed by powerful local men whose racist beliefs were well known.

On the evening of February 7, 1970, John and one of his associates at the community centre, Doug Huemmer, were driving to a meeting. They were arrested by a local deputy and taken to jail where they were beaten almost to the point of death. After languishing in jail for two days, they were finally rescued by friends. The attack was

meant to be a warning to John and the wider community to stop the civil rights activity and the challenge to the status quo. But John was even more
motivated to expand the Voice of Calvary outreach,
and to engage the larger white community as well.
At his trial, John was vindicated, and he offered forgiveness to those who had persecuted and beaten
him.[1]

John's original motivation to return to his home
community was a spiritual conviction and it repre-
sented a caring attitude toward those back in Mississippi. He had no obligation to return. In fact, doing
so was a risk to his wife and five children. Yet John
was compelled, so he went. His initial work was
strictly spiritual, focusing on Bible study and church
attendance; however, the daily realities of a segre-
gated culture provoked John in ways that he had
never imagined. Soon reaching out to the physical,
social, economic and political concerns of his community became a matter of justice that could not be
denied. John's initial generosity was on the way to
something bigger and even more sustainable—justice for a disenfranchised part of the community.
And as the fight for justice continued over many
years, he still retained the basic generosity that
prompted his pilgrimage in the first place.

Today, John has a national organization that

focuses on reconciliation, an urban development organization and ongoing work in Mississippi. In my conversations with John over the years, he is a faithful encourager and a model for those who pursue justice.

I believe there is a constant link between generosity and the pursuit of justice. Working together, they offer a powerful response to situations of injustice and poverty in our world. Some might argue that acts of generosity are an easy way out when compared to the greater challenges of seeking justice, but the failure is not in generosity. It is the unfortunate failure of the generous to see the connection with justice. Attacking one will not ensure the emergence of the other. Our world needs more generosity *and* it needs more justice. The challenge is to make the connection so that everyone sees generosity on the road to justice.

Generosity and justice affect people at the deepest personal level. Along with the fight for justice, there is the issue of justice meted out on behalf of those who have been victims of crime. Bruce Murakami was happily married to his wife, Cindy, for twenty years and living in Florida. They had three children, two older sons and an eleven-year-old daughter named Chelsea. On November 16, 1998, Cindy and Chelsea left in the family minivan to do some shopping. While pulling out from the shopping mall they were struck by a car that was speeding at close to 90 miles per hour. The minivan then struck another car, which exploded, and Cindy and Chelsea were trapped inside their vehicle. From a few blocks away, Bruce saw the smoke and followed it to discover that his wife and daughter were the casualties of this horrific accident.

After conflicting reports were given of the details of the accident, authorities refused to prosecute Justin Cabezas, the nineteen-year-old driver of the rented car that collided with the Murakami vehicle. Bruce was so incensed by this injustice that he quit his job, hired a lawyer and began his own investigation. He even tracked down witnesses who claimed they had seen Cabezas street racing.

Three years later, prosecutors filed charges of two counts of manslaughter. If found guilty, Justin could be sentenced to thirty years in prison. Some time later, Bruce Murakami met Justin Cabezas for the first time. Now twenty-three years of age, Justin broke down and wept, expressing his remorse and regret for what had happened. Bruce was taken by the young man's clean-cut appearance and his genuine grief and regret. He decided to change his actions.

Bruce responded to Justin by asking him to publicly apologize to his sons for the deaths in the family and to cooperate with him to warn other young people of the dangers of reckless driving. Later, at the trial, Bruce publicly forgave Justin and asked the judge not to send him to prison. He argued that it was important that something positive come out of this terrible tragedy. Justin Cabezas was sentenced to two years of probation and 300 hours of community service. Bruce and Justin now speak regularly about the dangers of reckless driving to high schools.

When asked why he did such a thing, Bruce Murakami says he believes that it is what his wife would have wanted. His comment reflects justice tempered by generosity. "It's exactly what she would have done, because of her faith and her compassion. We were together twenty years. She lived a good life and taught me well."[2]

By his example, Bruce has demonstrated the place of generosity and compassion in the midst of a horrible tragedy. The requirements of the state, the protection of the perpetrator and the demands of the victim influence justice. Bruce's willingness to step outside the more traditional response to a deep injustice has uplifted his life while redeeming the life of another.

Justice requires the accused to face the victim and be held to account. Our particular legal system is based on compensation and retribution. It may include everything from a financial payment to jail time. Yet there is a place for something that goes beyond the law and justice, and it's largely in the hands of the victim. It is the power to forgive.

The victim of a crime usually demands justice from the perpetrator. In fact the law requires such a transaction. Yet the line between justice and revenge is a thin one. Justice without generosity fulfills the legal requirements, but raises questions about healing and restoration, especially of the victim. It is an awkward discussion because it's difficult for anyone to judge the victim of a crime. She is right to be outraged. Anger is a human emotion that releases the venom in the deepest recesses of our emotional life and it protects us from self-destruction. Yet this very outrage, if unchecked, can dominate the life of a victim to such an extent that living is frozen around an event in the past. Unless a victim is able to move beyond the past horror, she can be paralyzed and unhappy for the rest of her life.

Generosity can be an attitude that sits comfortably with the pursuit of justice and it can be a significant factor in the healing process for victims and their loved ones. For the truly generous person, the only option is to look for opportunities to turn a devastating experience into a healing one.

Five years ago, the Anglican church that I attend in Streetsville, Ontario, was just months away from completing a major renovation. Trinity was a small church that was growing into a larger one. On the evening of April 27, 1998, three teenage boys broke into the building site and one of them threw a lighted match across a roll of tarpaper. The paper ignited and the boys panicked. Within seconds the flames lit up the skies and, by the time the firefighters arrived, there was little they could do. Our more than 150-year-old church was a smouldering, sickening mess. My wife, Diane, who is on staff at Trinity, described it as one of the most despairing experiences of her life.

Within a few days, the boys, who were not part of Trinity, had been located and the guilty party admitted his responsibility. Reaction among the Trinity congregation was mixed. Everyone was angry and upset. Some thought the boy should be prosecuted to the limit of the law, while others expressed more restraint. As the days and weeks progressed, our rector, Harold Percy, became convinced that this was an opportunity to go beyond justice and express mercy. After consulting with the leadership of the congregation and consulting an ethicist, he decided to push for a course of prosecution that was focused more on healing than retribution. Eventually the young man came to trial. After consultation with the prosecutors and the lawyer, some conditions were agreed upon. The sentence would not include incarceration, but the teenager would be required to do three things. First, he was to make a confession before the entire congregation. Second, he was to set up the portable chairs every Sunday at the school that was providing a temporary facility for our Sunday services. Third, he was to give 10 percent of the earnings from his part-time job as a donation to the church's rebuilding fund.

More than a year later, with our services still taking place in a local elementary school, the big Sunday arrived for the scheduled confession and apology. There were still mixed feelings in the congregation. Our rector had worked carefully with the proposed confession and had twice asked for it to be re-written. The young man's casual and over-confident attitude was less than encouraging; he explained that speaking in front of crowds was not a challenge since he had experience singing in a band with his friends. The young man's parents were sitting in the front row. After some congregational singing, the rector moved to the front and explained the arrangement that had been made following the church fire.

There was great tension in the room as the young man, now nineteen years old, moved to the lectern. He was hesitant, awkward and unsure. As he began to read, expressing his regret, he stumbled and began to cry. The self-assurance was gone and the brokenness was on display. The anguished apology stopped and started repeatedly. His mother wept in the foreground and in those moments there was an emotional shift both for the perpetrator and for those victimized. When he finished speaking there was a slight pause, an empty space in the air, and then the congregation began to applaud. It spread throughout the gathering of more than 600 people.

Later, members of the church came up to hug the young man, offer forgiveness and express their encouragement for his act of contrition and regret. There was an important transaction taking place. A church willing to express generosity and compassion in the midst of a devastating tragedy was seeing justice done through the eyes of forgiveness and reconciliation. Is this better justice than a judge exacting the maximum penalty and the convicted being institutionalized so that he can pay for his crime? Perhaps it is too early to tell. But the answer will be visible in both the outcome of this young man's life and the closure experienced by the Trinity congregation. Justice with generosity and compassion is a step of faith that grows out of the relationship between perpetrator and victim, and the belief that bringing something redemptive out of a criminal act is a greater good than retribution.

Justice and generosity have a special place when dealing with the poor. Charity, the willingness to give of one's time and money, is a traditional response to those who face want and neglect in a society. Offering food, shelter and other basics of life provides a lifeline for those who suffer. And generous charity—the kind that gives from a desire to help rather than from a sense of duty—is seen as an even better thing because it offers more to those who depend on it to stay alive.

Author Brennan Manning recounts a famous story of Mayor Fiorello LaGuardia in New York City during the depths of the Great Depression:

One bitterly cold night in January of 1935, the mayor turned up at a night court that served the poorest ward of the city. LaGuardia dismissed the judge for the evening and took over the bench himself. Within a few minutes, a tattered old woman was brought before him, charged with stealing a loaf of bread. She told LaGuardia that her daughter's husband had deserted her, her daughter was sick, and her two grandchildren were starving. But the shopkeeper, from whom the bread was stolen, refused to drop the charges. "It's a bad neighbourhood, your Honour," the man told the mayor. "She's got to be punished to teach other people around here a lesson."

LaGuardia sighed. He turned to the woman and said, "I've got to punish you. The law makes no exceptions—ten dollars or ten days in jail." But even as he pronounced the sentence, the mayor was already reaching into his pocket. He extracted a bill and tossed it into his famous sombrero saying: "Here is the ten dollar fine which I now remit; and furthermore I am going to fine everyone in this courtroom fifty cents for living in a town where a person has to steal bread so that her grandchildren can eat. Mr. Bailiff, collect the fines and give them to the defendant."

So the following day the New York City newspapers reported that $47.50 was turned over to a bewildered old lady who had stolen a loaf of bread to feed her starving grandchildren, fifty cents of that amount being contributed by the red-faced grocery store owner, while some seventy petty criminals, people with traffic violations, and New York City policemen, each of whom had just paid fifty cents for the privilege of doing so, gave the mayor a standing ovation.[3]

While justice certainly doesn't deny the need for generosity and charity, it raises some additional questions. The poor may be poor because they are denied things that are rightfully theirs. It is society's responsibility to ensure that they have meaningful employment, access to a good education, basic medical care, access to property ownership, the ability to secure a loan at reasonable interest and the right to vote for a representative government. Since securing this kind of justice is often a complicated, demanding task, doling out charity may in fact distract individuals and society from the more onerous, complicated task of ensuring justice.

In fact, some argue that generous charity is a kind of rationalizing of the existing circumstances that create injustice. When relating to the poor, for instance, it is more convenient to give a handout than to address the deeper causes that keep people poor. The former speaks to generosity and the latter speaks to justice. It's a tension that can separate the one from the other. And with the increasingly litigious nature of our society, perhaps it's time to bring these two virtues back together. Generosity without justice is a band-aid that offers one-time encouragement. Justice without generosity is a long-term solution that fails to heal the hearts of those who can make a difference. Together justice and generosity offer a powerful force that can change the world.

"I always knew that deep down in every human heart, there is mercy and generosity."

(Nelson Mandela)[1]

Chapter Seven

The Power of Generosity to Make Peace

In his Nobel Peace Prize acceptance speech, former U.S. President Jimmy Carter said, "How can we ever expect to find peace if we keep killing each other's children?" Revenge and violence are the carriers of the toxins that destroy peace and civility in a society. There can be no substantial change in a conflict unless both sides move away from a narrow self-interest point of view. The question becomes: who will make the first concession? Powerful forces behind the scenes are at work to encourage either generosity toward the other side or to build barriers that will separate and divide even further.

In conversation with the local people who are trapped in conflict situations, especially the poor, the majority favour peace in most situations. They simply want to get on with raising their children, harvesting their crops and doing business. Common sense tells us that in most cases it is an armed minority that wants to perpetuate the violence and the vindictiveness. In the post–9/11 world, this same phenomenon is challenging life in the West, especially the United States. The "war on terror" is similar, in some ways, to the Cold War paranoia of a few decades ago. How will nations avoid the temptation to see a terrorist behind every tree? The only alternative is to take a view of these difficult situations that goes beyond our most basic, fearful reactions. Somehow in the midst of violence and terror we are called to practise a generosity of spirit. We have to take risks based on the belief that making a positive gesture will open the way toward peace. If we fail to do so we diminish the very freedom and opportunity that we cherish.

Perhaps the greatest challenge to finding peace in the midst of conflict is the demand to look beyond the immediate situation. When hatred and violence are high, the credibility of peace is at its lowest. Being committed to peace means looking beyond the circumstances. Generosity increases our ability to see what is not readily apparent.

During a talk show interview on a local television station in Canada in 1999, a middle-aged woman and her twelve-year-old daughter shared the terror of losing three family members in the violence of India's ethnic and religious conflict. Some months earlier, missionary doctor Graham Staines, husband to Gladys and father to Esther, was attacked along with the couple's two sons, Philip, ten, and Timothy, eight, by an extremist Hindu mob. Their vehicle was set on fire and all three perished in the flames. Gladys and Esther avoided the tragedy because they had stayed at home in Baripada, many miles from the tragic incident.

Some months later a Hindu radical named Dara Singh and ten of his supporters were arrested and accused of the murders. Gladys Staines announced that she had forgiven the killers and delivered a message of tolerance and religious harmony to the entire nation. Subsequently she and her daughter returned to their native Australia for a lengthy furlough and recovery. Today, both Gladys and Esther are back in India. Gladys is operating the leprosy clinic previously managed by her husband and Esther is a student at Hebron Academy in South India.

Last year in recognition of her work for peace, Gladys Staines received the prestigious Gandhi Communal Harmony award. She was one of three recipients, each from a different religion. Upon receiving the award Gladys commented, "I accepted the award because it was for communal harmony. That is the need of the hour."

Compassion, forgiveness, generosity and her Christian faith appear to be at the heart of this incredible witness. In spite of her heartbreak and sadness, Gladys was drawn by a transcendent purpose that looks beyond the current situation to see another opportunity to help and care. Her genuine commitment to reach out to others lifted her out of the temptation to self-pity and despair. Gladys' generous spirit saw opportunity rather than defeat. This is a dramatic example of generosity's power to make peace.

In contrast to the dramatic and heavily publicized nature of Gladys Staines' witness, seemingly small gestures of generosity can sometimes have consequences beyond imagining. Former South African Anglican Archbishop Trevor Huddleston tells of one such story. He once belonged to a church that operated a school where the young Desmond Tutu was a student. On one occasion, Huddleston visited Desmond's home and was introduced to his mother. Rev. Huddleston raised his hat and said, "How do you do, Mrs. Tutu?" It was the first time Desmond had ever seen a white man raise his hat to an African woman. Later he recalled this experience as one of the things that would lead him to the Anglican priesthood. And, of course, years later, Archbishop Desmond Tutu would become one of the leaders to speak out against apartheid while appealing for peace, justice and reconciliation. Huddleston's small act of courtesy had a small but direct influence on rescuing South Africa from its difficult past.

Generosity is also a factor in the larger and more obvious peace issues as well. In his autobiography, *Long Walk to Freedom*, Nelson Mandela documents the key steps in the move to full freedom for all the people of South Africa. While maintaining his dignity and passion for justice, he demonstrated a generosity of spirit that became an essential ingredient in the formation of a new government. While still in prison, Mandela initiated secret meetings with the apartheid government. When some of his African National Congress (ANC) colleagues questioned his willingness to make the first move in pursuing these meetings, Mandela was clear about the importance of taking the first step. His comments to an ANC colleague reflect both generosity to his opponents and a willingness to take a risk. "I replied that if he was not against negotiations in principle, what did it matter who initiated them? What mattered was what they achieved, not how they started. I told Walter that I thought we should move forward with negotiations and not worry about who knocked on the door first."[2] Subsequent events proved Mandela absolutely right. His willingness to take the first step set a pattern of negotiations that ended in freedom for the black and coloured majority of South Africa. A generous attitude often becomes the first step in building trust, and without it, peace is impossible.

Later in his book Mandela speaks powerfully about what he believes to be essential in relations with others. "I always knew that deep down in every human heart, there is mercy and generosity. No one is born hating another person because of the colour of his skin, or his background or his religion. People must learn to hate, and if they can learn to hate, they can be taught to love, for love comes more naturally to the human heart than its opposite. Even in the grimmest times in prison, when my comrades and I were pushed to the limits, I would see a glimmer of humanity in one of the guards, perhaps just for a second, but it was enough to reassure me and keep me going. Man's goodness is a flame that can be hidden but never extinguished."[3]

Now, years later, Mandela has retired from political office, but his generous spirit is still a backdrop of hope and possibility that shines brightly in the nation of South Africa. The power of his message has become a beacon of hope to people everywhere.

In sharp contrast to the South African experience, Israel and Palestine continue their violent attacks against each other. Both sides recite the outrages of the other, justifying the need for more violence. For the Palestinians the rhetoric is fashioned around justice and oppression; for Israel it's the call for protection against a foe committed to their destruction. Day after day, death after death, the march toward a final showdown continues. There is no room for generosity. Each side plays to the worst caricature of the other. The result is that two peoples are being torn apart. Lives will continue to be lost, and some day, when peace does come, long after the leaders and perpetrators of the worst violence are gone, many will think, "why did we wait so long?"

Generosity is not the panacea for all of life's problems, but its expression is at the heart of successful peacemaking. Peacemaking depends on trust, and trust begins with expressions of generosity whether tangible or intangible. It takes these small steps and a generous spirit to begin the journey of peace.

Our former president at World Vision, Dr. Stan Mooneyham, told me of his experience of leading a Latin American church leaders conference in the 1980s. It was an assemblage of leaders from every persuasion—Catholic, Protestant, conservative, liberationist—and the first day began, filled with arguments and disagreements. Stan wished that someone else had the role of facilitating this disparate group.

The next day he went to the flip chart and put a series of isolated dots on a fresh sheet of paper. He drew a small circle around each dot and explained that's how he had felt the day before: each person had drawn a little dot around himself for protection. Then, in a grand gesture, Stan drew a large circle that circumscribed the entire page and quoted from Edwin Markham's famous poem.

He drew a circle that shut me out—
Heretic, rebel, a thing to flout,
But Love and I had the wit to win:
We drew a circle that took him in.[4]

Then Stan commented, "I may not be in your circle, but you are in mine, and there is nothing you can do to get out. You can't resign, walk out, or run away. If you try it, I will just draw a bigger circle."[5]

The tension in the room dissipated as Stan explained how God's love draws a circle that includes the entire world, and asked how members in this smaller group could do anything less. The remainder of the conference resulted in some of the best relationship building and discussion that World Vision has ever experienced.

I have seen generosity and peacemaking join together in some of the most difficult situations imaginable. The pace can be slow and halting, yet there are dramatic examples of ordinary people who make a profound difference. Deborah Nyirakabirikira was a mother who had survived the genocide in Rwanda, Africa, in 1994. Along with the rest of her country, she was trying to put her life together again after the killing and violence. Deborah's husband had been killed, so she relied heavily on her eleven children. One son, nineteen-year-old Innocent, was a special source of joy and satisfaction in a life that had been framed by death and disappointment.

Being a woman of deep faith, Deborah had a practice of praying every morning in the back room of her small house. In April 1997 she had been troubled by a vision that Innocent was going to be killed. Deborah felt so strongly about this devastating image that she shared it with Innocent. She recalls that they even spent time together discussing and praying about this. On a subsequent evening, after Innocent had cooked a meal for the family, some soldiers came to the door and asked for Innocent. They explained that they wanted to ask him some questions, and assured her they would not kill him.

Shortly after leaving with the soldiers Innocent returned to his mother and said to her, "Mummy, they are going to kill me." She embraced him, but the soldiers pulled them apart, and minutes later Deborah heard the gunshots that took her son's life. At Innocent's funeral, she was overcome by grief and questioned how God could allow such a tragedy. In spite of her emotional and intellectual struggles, she continued her practice of prayer and meditation. On one of these occasions Deborah had a vision that showed a house built on a bridge across a deep chasm. The only way across the chasm was through this house. Below the house were these words: "The way to heaven is through the house of your enemy."

Deborah was comforted by the people from her church, her faith in God and an overwhelming sense that something redemptive was to come from this tragedy. Some weeks later, three soldiers came to her door. Her first thought was that they had come to kill her. Then one soldier, whom she recognized from the previous visit, stepped forward and led her by the shoulder into the sitting room. He closed the door, and Deborah expected to be killed. Instead he turned to her and said, "Pray for me." They got down on their knees together and she began to pray for him.

After the prayer, the soldier said, "My name is Charles," and began to cry. Charles admitted that he was the one who had killed her son as the result of Innocent telling the authorities about a theft he had been involved in. As time had passed he had felt increasingly guilty and despondent. He said to Deborah, "Would you forgive me? If not, take me to court and I am prepared to be killed for my crime, because this is the law."

Deborah was stunned at first and then began to pray for direction. Her response would become part of Rwanda's healing. She remembered the strange vision and the words "the way to heaven is through the house of your enemy." Deborah told this young man that she was prepared to forgive him. She had no desire to turn him in to the authorities because he would simply rot in jail and eventually be executed. She had already lost her son; there was no reason to lose another young man.

In re-telling this story, Deborah explains how her memory of the vision and the words of forgiveness in the Bible began to overwhelm her. She hugged Charles and they began to cry. Deborah describes how a great burden had been lifted from them, even though it was very hard. She told Charles, "The only punishment I can inflict on you is to take you in place of my son and to feed you the food I would have given my son." Charles turned to her and said, "I am your child now. I will visit you whenever I can."

In the months and years that have followed, Deborah has shared this experience with the wider community in Rwanda, and many have found her example an essential step in learning to forgive. Deborah comments on the difference in her town. "Ruhengiri is now a different place. The killings have stopped, the Interahamwe [the genocidal paramilitaries] are gone and peace has returned to my beautiful corner of Rwanda. I am proud to have played a small part in bringing this about."[6]

In a country where an estimated one million people died in genocide, Deborah's witness is an important contribution to healing and reconciliation. In this extraordinary story, numerous elements of generosity, forgiveness and compassion form a fabric of reconciliation that is impossible to separate. Generosity is an attitude that affects each of the other elements. Deborah was willing to think the unthinkable and consider the impossible. She was willing to step outside the world of her own grave injustice and consider an alternative. Her religious faith challenged the prevailing paradigm of an eye for an eye and a life for a life. In stories like these, there is a willingness to give up the need for payback. Like others I have met, Deborah came to the realization that if she did not forgive she would be burdened with anger and the desire for revenge for the rest of her life. The generosity to the perpetrator is matched by the victim's wish to be free of the insidious, paralyzing despair that would inevitably follow vengeance.

Deborah also discovered that all of Charles' immediate family had been murdered during the genocide. His future was filled with anger and retribution: it could have been a mirror of hers.

Deborah's willingness to look outside herself enabled her to look into another person's pain, even though she was from a different ethnic clan in Rwanda. Generosity reflects an attitude toward life that enhances the possibility of seeing others as you see yourself. The needs of others become a reflection of the wants and desires that rest deep in the emotional and spiritual life of every person.

As Rwanda continues its slow journey back to harmony and reconciliation, its political leaders are using a judicial approach that releases those judged of lesser genocidal crimes back to their local villages where they will confess and work toward reconciliation. It's a grand experiment in human dynamics as well as justice, generosity and reconciliation. In a small country where thousands have confessed their complicity in genocidal crime, it is the only practical way forward. Deborah is one of many who are determined to break free from the demons of the past and live in a different way. She is helping to create the hope that is the salvation of a country carrying the burden of mass killing and hatred.

Peacemaking, whether in our own personal relationships or in the wider community, requires an attitude of generosity. Small actions take on great significance. The willingness to take risk is critical. It's also clear that the parties involved must be open to a different future—one filled with hope rather than vengeance. The natural desire to strike back will perpetuate the anger and hostilities between both parties. Pushing aside the past hurts to concentrate on the new future is what makes peacemaking possible.

"I have found the paradox that if I love until it hurts, then there is no hurt, but only more love."

(Mother Teresa)

Chapter Eight

The Power of Generosity: What Lies Behind?

Where does generosity come from? What motivates it? Surely, generosity does not rise out of a vacuum. As a virtue, it must be connected to some deeper beliefs or motivations. As a Christian, my commitment to generosity is intimately connected to my religious beliefs. Christianity sees life itself as a generous gift from God. The coming of Jesus and his subsequent death and resurrection demonstrate the next chapter in God's generosity. He set an example for everyone to follow. My faith, then, is at the very heart of my belief in generosity. Other people practising generosity will point to their faith in Judaism, Islam, Buddhism or Hinduism as the foundation for their behaviour, while still others hold to an ideology or philosophy rather than a religious belief.

Because I am an activist, I have to discipline myself to push back and think about these deeper motivations, otherwise the activity itself becomes the fuel for my generosity. And experience has taught me that one activity after another will not carry the heavy freight of generosity. It must go deeper. Otherwise life is one frenetic, adrenalin-fuelled emergency after another. Too often the tyranny of the urgent undermines the necessity for time and reflection to feed the soul.

Self-criticism and spiritual direction are steps to ensure that our humanitarian intent doesn't damage others or ourselves. The highway of helping is littered with human lives that have been burned out and destroyed by the incessant pressure to do more for others while neglecting personal disciplines and responsibilities. Without these safeguards, negotiating the potholes of temptation and the despair of failure will overwhelm even the most generous spirit.

In Zambia, I toured a small, three-sided building in a slum community. It was filled with 150

HIV/AIDS–affected children ranging in age from four to twelve. Local teachers volunteered to teach these children in four two-hour shifts each day. Most of the children were orphans, meaning they had lost either both parents or their mother. It was hot, cramped and crowded and most of the children were very energetic. Their boisterous songs were filled with energy. Four of the older children stepped out and began brief recitations about the AIDS pandemic in their country. They spoke of the danger, the need to be careful, the importance of abstinence and their hope for the future. It was all a wonderful reminder that Africa is not giving up in the midst of this crisis.

I noticed a small form at the back of the group. It was a four-year-old boy named Royde. He was gaunt. Even his dark skin was ashen. But it was his eyes that pierced my heart. He was staring ahead yet looking nowhere. I called the teacher over and asked her to give me his story. She explained that he was an orphan who was living with his uncle. It was obvious that he wasn't getting enough to eat. His diminished condition spoke more clearly than words. Royde said he had had some sour milk the day before—that was all.

While taking notes on this situation I was distracted and taken to interview another child, then another and another. Soon I was asked to speak with the local leaders. World Vision had no work in this part of the city, so we were being challenged to get involved. Our Zambian staff were concerned because we were already over-committed. Soon I was taken to the car and whisked off to a flight back to the capital city of Lusaka. The evening finished with meetings and there were more meetings the next morning; it was a whirlwind of activity. Finally, I was back on a plane to Canada. My wife, Diane, who wasn't feeling well, was sitting next to me in the rear section of a full-up Boeing 747. It was late at night and she had fallen asleep for some needed rest.

Suddenly in the darkened airplane I could see the face of little Royde. The exhausted look on his face began to break my heart. I remembered that I had done nothing to provide immediate help for this forgotten boy. I was too busy and taken up with too many things. As I recalled his face, the neglect, and the raw, unbridled need for the basics to stay alive, I began to cry. The lights were out; the tears were rolling down my cheeks. Here I was, a veteran of nearly thirty years in humanitarian work, and I didn't even take the time to ensure that a little suffering boy was cared for. All the big things had crowded out the most important thing, so I wept.

Sometimes it's all I can do as a broken, bumbling member of the human race.

And then, after a while, I feel God's grace, a reminder that I'm forgiven, not destroyed; accountable, not lost. In that redemptive moment on the plane I mapped out a plan to get some aid to that boy with the help of my Zambian colleagues. To fail is human; not to try is the devil.

Our desire to be generous is strong, but it is also fragile because the need around us is so great. The relentless pressure to act draws us into more and more responsibility. If we lose our emotional balance, we are like a tightrope walker pushing an overloaded wheelbarrow. Eventually everything, including the walker, the wheelbarrow and the load, will fall. One corrective is to have realistic expectations. We can only do so much.

I also believe it's critical to ensure that the relational aspect of helping people is not neglected. There must be time to listen, dialogue and respond on an individual basis. Dealing with leadership issues, looking at the big picture and engaging with the major issues and systems that keep people poor is important, but we are fuelled at the deepest levels by personal relationships. We do this because we care for people, one by one. My moment of truth is the realization that coping with all the demands of a humanitarian job is not as important as relating to children and adults on an individual basis. It always leads me back to those simple, essential beliefs that frame my life and my vocation. Neglecting them is a sure way to end up defeated and discouraged. Even generosity cannot run on empty. The fuel comes from people and a power that is much bigger than me.

An Iranian movie called *Baran* tells the wonderful story of a teenager who discovers the nature of love and generosity. Lateef works at a construction site providing the lunches and tea breaks to a construction crew in Tehran. Most of the workers are Afghanis in the country illegally. Lateef is boisterous and strong-willed, but looked after by a relative who has given him this job. In a pointless bout of temper Lateef gets into a fight and loses his cushy job and is reassigned to carry the heavy bricks for construction. Much to his anger, a younger boy is given his old job. Lateef does everything he can to make this lad's job a misery. He destroys cutlery, upsets trays, trips him and steals food. Still the new boy cooks and serves better, and the workers grow in their appreciation of him. Intrigued by this, Lateef steals into the cooking area and discovers that this boy is actually a young woman in disguise, named Baran. Unaware, she has let down her hair and is brushing it very carefully. It's an epiphany for Lateef.

He is smitten with the beautiful young woman, and his entire attitude changes. Lateef tries to be near her, looks out for her and offers assistance wherever he can. When the local immigration authorities make a surprise raid, Lateef manages to interfere with the officials so that the girl escapes. Baran loses her job and Lateef spends prodigious amounts of time trying to find her. Eventually he finds her at the edge of a slum community. Lateef is too shy to show himself, so he hides himself behind a bridge pylon. He watches the girl along with other Afghani women retrieving rocks from the middle of the river in the wintertime. It is physically numbing, inhuman work. The girl slips under the heavy rock she is carrying and is only saved because the other women retrieve her before she is washed down the river.

Lateef is beside himself, almost leaping to the rescue before he realizes such an action would break the traditions that separate them. So he stands broken, hidden from view, with tears streaming down his cheeks. His emotions are a blend of love, compassion and generosity unexpressed. He is in agony—full of vicarious suffering that is tender and fragile.

Later Lateef learns the girl's family needs to return to Afghanistan. He sells his most prized possession, his worker registration card, and gives the money to the girl's father so they can return to Afghanistan. Lateef helps them load the broken-down truck that will take them home. In the final goodbye, one of the girl's shoes gets stuck in the mud. Lateef retrieves it for her. The truck rattles down the slum passageway, while Lateef watches the small shoe print slowly wash away in the rain.[1]

Lateef was a lout, focused only on his own selfish desires, when suddenly he saw a person in a new light. The preoccupation with self was turned inside out. Generous acts of kindness became his daily goal. Looking outside himself, even to a relationship that must remain at a distance, transformed his attitude toward others. Expressing love and generosity is more than doing things; it is finding something in ourselves that longs to be expressed. Whether it's the first love of a teenager, the opportunity to offer a meal or the simple gesture of opening the door for someone, our interior life is fed and renewed. It is these personal connections that make generosity so powerful and important. In all our busyness, generosity is first and foremost personal, based on human relationships and fuelled by our desire to connect and make a difference. The power of generosity is the transformation it brings to both the giver and the receiver.

One of my heroes is Stephen Lewis, the Canadian statesman who has served as a politician, diplomat, professor and senior UN representative. At an age when many people slip into a comfortable retirement, Stephen accepted an appointment by the UN Secretary-General to be the Special Envoy for HIV/AIDS in Africa. When he began, it was a thankless, monumental task. The statistics of death and destruction were horrific, and moving toward an epidemic. Stephen became a gadfly who cajoled, coerced, advocated and pressed relentlessly for the world to pay attention to this human catastrophe. Slowly the world has begun to pay attention and Stephen's generous gifts of time and energy are making a difference. He jokingly describes himself as a philistine and not religious, but his social democrat ideology and his commitment to humanitarianism infuse his unconditional passion for the unfortunate in Africa. When pressed about his motivation, Stephen defers to the courage and perseverance of the African people. His consistent actions match his powerful words. The experience of living and working in Africa as a university student first opened his eyes to these extraordinary people.

The Power of Generosity

Most cannot operate at the level of brilliance demonstrated by Stephen Lewis, but generosity is no respecter of persons or status. It is the attitude of caring combined with the willingness to share that makes generosity available to anyone. From the bricklayer to the UN diplomat, from the aid worker to the child in primary school, generosity is fuelled by beliefs and values greater than ourselves. Like any virtue, generosity cannot run on empty.

"If I'm clutching on to my money with both hands,
how can I be free to hug my wife and kids?"
(David Robinson, NBA All-Star)

"Charity does not like arithmetic; selfishness
worships it."

(Mason Cooley)

Chapter Nine

The Power of Generosity: Money

A serious discussion about generosity can't avoid
the place of money. In cultures that worship the
almighty dollar, generosity becomes both suppli-
cant and critic. We always need more of it, but we
need to be sure we want it for the right reasons.
The Bill and Melinda Gates Foundation has assets
worth forty billion dollars designated for charity,
and Canadian billionaire Ken Thomson in Canada

recently bestowed 270 million dollars on the Art Gallery of Ontario. Both are examples of wealthy individuals practising generosity at a substantial level. Almost every working day, I read letters from ordinary people who want to give money to assist those in need. Of course, being generous is about more than money; it involves our time, influence and expertise as well. But money stands higher in public perception than anything else.

Money is a reflection of our deepest motivations. Where your money is, there is your heart. Tracking how people spend their money is one of the most informative ways to determine the nature of a person's character. To deny the place of money in our world would be naive at best and downright dishonest at worst. Does this make money more important than anything else?

Money brings stability because everyone needs it and wants it. Money is a resource that provides food, shelter and clothing. It's a human construct that gives order to the exchange of things that we value. In our capitalist world, it's the only way to get on and get along. But there is a difference between a rightful place in our lives and one that dominates and becomes obsessive. Money can be part of the problem or part of the solution.

In one of the ethnic religious communities in

Toronto, a man was arrested and accused of taking millions of dollars from individuals who thought they were investing in a miracle teeth-whitening product that would reap huge returns. It was all a scam. Many invested their life savings and now they have nothing to show for it. Money was a vehicle to cheat and defraud. At about the same time in Winnipeg, I was involved in an event that raised one million dollars for the HIV/AIDS crisis in Africa. Money was a vehicle for hope and compassion. The intent and motivation was the opposite of the fraud case.

Money is a tool, not an end in itself. Author Michael Adams comments, "In modern societies, money displaces secular and religious power as the principal medium of exchange."[1] On the one hand it serves the intent of those who use it as a tool and on the other it brings some baggage because of what it stands for. Money gets worshipped as something that in itself will bring satisfaction and fulfillment. The tool suddenly becomes the prized possession instead of a step in a process that leads to a fulfilled life. This choice faces everyone. The Bible says you cannot serve God and money. (Luke 16:13) Whether you believe in God or not, the statement is making a point that you cannot have a transcendent value in your life while still holding money of equal importance. You have to make a choice. Your ultimate value will come in conflict with your desire to gain and hold money at all costs. At the fundraiser in Winnipeg, one family decided that they would match every single dollar contributed. Their ultimate value was to practise generosity and compassion because of their Christian faith. It superseded their desire to hold on to the money. Money became an important tool in their practice of generosity, however it was always secondary to the values that motivate their lives.

Some people have a gift for making money. I'm convinced that it's similar to one who is a gifted runner, a great singer, a talented musician or a spell-binding speaker. In their particular area of excellence, they see things differently; they have an intuitive knowledge or a physical attribute that gives them advantages to do this particular activity very well. When it comes to making money, however, along with skill, wisdom and intuition, there is an element of timing. How many fortunes have been made because someone stumbled onto the right product, the right delivery system, or the right advertising at the right time? Those of us with gifts in other areas need to remember this important lesson. How much money has been wasted in get-rich schemes for the average person? Most of those who are making money from these schemes are those who promote them. Shortcuts usually don't work out. So if generosity depends on lots of people making huge fortunes, we are in deep trouble. Fortunately, it doesn't work that way. Money as an end in itself becomes destructive, because it does not address the deep needs that make life truly meaningful and satisfying. The love of money is called greed and it destroys rather than builds anything of lasting value.

For most of us, being honest, learning a valued skill or profession, showing up and doing a competent job will give us enough to live comfortably, and it's still possible to be generous. There is a difference between what I want and what I really need. While our culture is screaming at us that we have to have more, our ultimate values are whispering in our ear to pursue only those things that are consistent with what we really want to become. My favourite reminder is: what will people have to say about me at my funeral? The money means very little. It's much more an issue of what we invest in people, especially in our families, our children and our communities. If you live well and rightly, you can have a great funeral.

In the frequent media mention of the cheaters, the unscrupulous and the dishonest, we lose sight of the majority of people who want to live by a set of values and practices that put money in its proper perspective. Working on behalf of a charity, I see generosity every day that shows the concern and compassion of hundreds of thousands of people. Yes, we are all influenced by an inescapable pressure to spend more on ourselves, but there is an offsetting persistence that keeps things in perspective. When people see there is a need and they can make a difference, they will respond. Generosity is not lost; compassion is not discarded, because most of us realize that if you go back far enough, all of us benefited from someone who helped us in a way that was not required. Generosity pays dividends.

Along the way I've learned some best practices with money that have cultivated my generosity. Everyone has to find their own way on this journey, but here is some counsel that you might find helpful. Always carry enough money in your pocket so that you can give a quick encouragement to someone in need. If you don't like cash, carry a blank cheque. Not only does this prepare you for emergencies, but it also encourages an attitude of compassionate paying attention. I'm not suggesting handouts, but simply a gesture to a friend or someone who is struggling. It reminds me that I'm on a mission of generosity and encouragement wherever it strikes me.

Panhandlers on the street can provoke the greatest challenge to those wishing to be generous with money. What is my responsibility? Unless I know the person's specific situation I will keep the amounts small. One friend, Dale, told me that before his daily trip to the city he prepares a duplicate sandwich to his own, which he gives to a street person at lunch time. He does a good deed and enjoys his own lunch more because he knows someone now has a meal like his.

Tom Caldwell, Chairman of Caldwell Securities Ltd., wraps a two-dollar coin in small-print portions of the Bible and hands them out to street people as he travels across the city. As someone who was rescued from the debilitation and destruction of alcoholism, Tom says it was generosity, but even more importantly the message in the Bible, that saved his life. Each of us in our own way brings our history to an act of generosity.

What we leave after we die can be a testament to generosity as well. My wife and I have prepared our wills so that our children are required to give away 10 percent of our estate to charities of their choice. While they will gain from the modest estate we leave behind, we are ensuring that they practise our commitment to generosity even at death. We hope it will also be a celebration for them to spend some time together giving something away. Our children have observed us as a couple at our best and worst times, but we believe that our commitment of generosity has weathered the storms and it will stick to them as well.

Find some organizations that you really believe in and give them your support. Whether it's a church, temple or charity, pass it on. You will have the satisfaction of knowing that you can make a difference. Giving away our money is one of the things that proves our humanity. Keeping more for ourselves is the natural thing to do, yet it fails to address the deepest yearning to bring significance to our lives. We are not creatures scattered by chance in a world of random relationships. We can make choices. We can influence our world. Last year, I was in Tanzania and met a woman who is HIV-positive. She is a dedicated counsellor to those who are suffering just like her. I asked her why she did this work, when she had a full-time job just staying alive. With a passion that startled me, she said, "I finally decided that I'm not dead yet and God has a plan for the rest of my life, so I decided to get involved." Hers is an act of faith, but the odds are in her favour.

One neglected concept holds a powerful secret about money—tithing. This idea comes out of the Old Testament writings from the time of Moses.

Tithing refers to a practice of giving back to church or temple 10 percent of your earnings each year. The concept was based on the idea that everything belongs to God so you should give at least 10 percent back to the work of God. It became a measure of pure devotion. I'm convinced that this practice is relevant to anyone who wants to steward his or her life in the most meaningful way possible. Why? Tithing is a great way to help those less fortunate or marginalized in society. You can really be part of something substantial if you give away 10 percent.

Tithing teaches the value of money. Most of us can't give away 10 percent without diminishing our lifestyle. Tithing consistently reminds us of our values, and challenges us to sort out our priorities. What are we really prepared to invest our money in? Tithing also teaches the right use of money. If you are giving away 10 percent rather than ten dollars here and there, you are much more likely to do your homework and make sure you are investing your regular giving into something that really does make a difference in people's lives.

Tithing teaches discipline. It won't happen unless you hold yourself accountable. There has to be a plan as well as commitment. All the surveys show that most people lack intentionality and discipline when it comes to handling personal finances.

Tithing pushes us to climb that mountain in our lives and make some decisions.

Tithing also sets an incredible example for our children. Family discussions around priorities and the commitment to help others establish a foundation of compassion and generosity that will affect our children for the rest of their lives. There are moments of real learning when you delay a major purchase or postpone a holiday because of a commitment to help others. Our children may whine and fuss, but, believe me, they get the point.

Yet, in our family's experience, I have been truly amazed at how seldom we miss the money we give away. In fact, there have been numerous occasions when money shows up at just the right time to meet an unexpected need. I have been tithing every year for more than thirty years. It works. Another piece of advice: if you want to find someone who cares about others and follows through on assignments, find a tither.

Finally, tithing is about legacy—what are we leaving behind? Relationships, values and practice are the stuff of who we are. Money is a reflection of those commitments in our lives. Giving our money away contributes to building a future of hope and possibility. It doesn't just happen; it takes generous people.

But maybe you're saying, "Give me a break: I

don't go to a church, and tithing is only for religious fanatics. Besides, the government should be looking after these needs." Well, it isn't happening. Even the most cursory review of government services shows the safety net is shrinking. There are more and more people in profound need. And nobody is breaking down the government's doors to increase taxes. So if generous people don't come to the table we ensure ourselves an increasingly precarious future of worsening human disaster and greater fragmentation of our society.

If you don't go to church, temple or mosque, then practise your 10 percent generosity giving on charities that address the needs of your community, country and the world. The range of significant charitable work being accomplished is more than most people imagine—everything from providing small, low-interest loans to the poor to life-saving health and food initiatives that address the needs of hungry children here and overseas. Connect with organizations that have a reputation for transparency and effective work. They should be audited regularly and their financial information should be available to anyone.

. . .

There are people who oppose most of the principles I have suggested about money. They live for money and they will use every technique and subterfuge to get what they want. Such single-minded greed can take the breath away. So you and I have a choice to make. We must go to the well of our deepest beliefs and decide what kind of person we want to become. There is a decision to be made and a cost to be paid.

Every decision carries a risk, but each of us can decide what will gain our allegiance. My choice is one based on hard work, honesty, earned value, fair wages and generosity. Without these values, life for our society is grim, for they bring hope, goodwill and stability. Yes, the greedy and unscrupulous may get public adulation for their single-minded achievement, even underscored by an occasional generous public gift, but what lives inside their hearts? Is it a place where I want to live?

We have to decide whether we want to be like rats fleeing a sinking ship, each one for himself, scavenging whatever he can carry and grab, ignoring his neighbours in pursuit of dry land and a place to feather his nest. Or are we part of a human family created in the image of God that is building a way of life based on generosity, justice and a level playing field? In these days of extravagant payments to some senior executives as well as the commonly touted belief that everyone can and should run to the trough of greed and free lunches, the call for moral and ethical values seems quaint and out of touch. Yet the bell still tolls for those who want to make this world a better place for everybody. Should the day come when our civilization crashes, the prophets standing on the watchtowers won't ask for more greed and self-interest, they will lament the loss of generosity, diligence and justice—a fitting eulogy to a country and people who lost their way.

"Come to me, all you that are weary and are carrying heavy burdens, and I will give you rest. Take my yoke upon you, and learn from me; for I am gentle and humble in heart, and you will find rest for your souls. For my yoke is easy, and my burden is light."

(Matthew 11:28–30, NRSV)

Chapter Ten

Failure: A Personal Testimony

Practising generosity is risky, because you expect good things of yourself. Higher expectations can be accompanied by as much failure as success. One goes with the other. Yet experiencing failure is often the best way to grow. Our stumbling becomes the pathway to greater opportunity for life-enriched experience. Perhaps better said—screwing up and failing forward. In my experiences as a humanitarian worker, compassion and generosity are no insurance against deep personal failure.

I have had the disappointment and despair of seeing some of the evidence of the great killing machines of the past thirty-some years. It began with the atrocities in the 1970s committed in Uganda, East Africa, by the government of Idi Amin. I can still recall the stench and blood on the wall of the State Research Bureau in the capital city, Kampala. There were strands of human hair scattered in the humid, dark underground basement. It was a favourite location to torture confessions out of political opponents and ordinary citizens. In the countryside, there were piles of skulls where the killers had wreaked havoc on the local population. It was vengeful, vicious and unrelenting. Uganda still bears the scars from that period more than two decades ago.

On the other side of the world in Southeast Asia, Cambodia was reeling from its own brand of inhumanity. "Year Zero" was the starting point for the Marxist Khmer Rouge. In their arrogance they believed they could re-create Cambodian society based on their purist political ideology. Education, wearing glasses or any indications of Western influence cost people their lives. It's estimated that one million people were killed by this vicious mix of ideology and hatred.

In 1984, I was in Ethiopia witnessing a drought and food shortage that would take hundreds of thousands of lives. Television documented the daily starvation of children on a scale never broadcast before. The Western public was horrified by what they saw. Individuals, governments and international agencies joined together in one of the most dramatic responses in history, yet it was too late for so many children and adults. Doctors and nurses were often placed in the heart-wrenching position of determining who would get food and who wouldn't. Children with matchstick arms and legs filled all available emergency shelters while staff stretched resources beyond the limit. The choice was life for some and death for others. The outside world had failed to pay attention to the developing catastrophe in a faraway country, and now starving children were paying the ultimate price.

A decade later, in 1994, I was no stranger to the failure of generosity and human decency. But nothing fully prepared me for the experience of the genocide and destruction in Rwanda, Central Africa. The greatest enemy of generosity is the despair that accompanies the indiscriminate murder of people or the neglect that ensures others will not survive. Rwanda and neighbouring Zaire (now known as the Democratic Republic of the Congo) provided the locations for both realities. It was the first time that I failed in a dramatic way to live up to the expectations of my calling as a humanitarian worker. My ability to act with generosity, compassion and competence was compromised in a way that I had never experienced.

In July 1994, Rwandans were fleeing by the tens of thousands to Zaire. Their plight was precipitated by their ethnic identity as Rwandan Hutus, since Hutus were charged with the vast majority of the genocidal killings in Rwanda. Now that the Rwandan Patriotic Front, dominated by the ethnic Tutsi group, was taking over government, the Hutus were fearful of retribution, so they fled. They were camping out on hillsides that were mostly volcanic rock covered by a thin layer of soil at best. Water was limited. There had been little time for preparation and the international community was reacting slowly. Dehydration and hunger were the chief killers, especially among the children. The ground was so hard that there was no immediate way to bury the hundreds dying every day. Each morning corpses of young and old were laid out in the refugee camps or along the roadside waiting for the trucks to collect them and move them to a mass burial site. I still recall the horror of seeing one of these trucks unload its cargo, bodies sliding out in a twisted collection of arms and legs and crumpling into a mass grave. This heartbreaking moment recalled genocide images from the Second World War in Europe.

What does generosity have to do with such a situation? We have long left the territory of generosity. A little shred of human dignity would be enough. Virtues of any kind are absent—blood, death and tears remain. I will never forget the confusion, the helplessness, the moral turmoil and the apocalyptic scene befitting a Dürer woodcut. A letter to my wife, Diane, replayed the hopelessness and the disappointment of my own response.

27 July 1994
Mugunga Camp, Goma, Zaire

Dear Diane,

It was a bad day and a good day in Goma, Zaire, among the Rwanda refugees. It was a bad day because I saw a man with no hope crawl to his death. I was on a hurried trip to discover the latest developments in our World Vision food distribution program at Mugunga Camp when it happened. The medical tents were off to the right as I climbed the modest rise into the camp. On the left-hand side, bodies were laid out like cord wood, all along the narrow roadway. When I passed the medical tents there were more bodies on the left. The sight and the stench take your breath away in the hot African sun.

Then, not more than four metres in front of me, a shrouded figure was crawling on his hands and knees toward an empty space in the line of corpses. A boy of about twelve had his hand on this crawling, macabre figure, while his face registered a stunned shock and silence. The shrouded form of the man collapsed at the empty space in the line, and died. Here was the most shocking, compelling tribute to death in this hell on earth.

It was a bad day because a woman among the thousands thrust the baby in her arms in front of me and said, "Help," and in my helplessness to do anything, I turned away. Even in the microcosm of one little life I could do nothing. I was afraid and the stench of hopelessness covered me, too. Right now I feel dirty and empty because I am a human being who is part of the despair and tragedy of this place.

It was a good day because I helped carry and transport six critically ill children from our Unaccompanied Children's Centre. We took them by car to the recently installed Israeli field hospital outside of Goma where we were met with generosity and true professionalism. The hospital staff attacked the illnesses trying to take these children's lives with a single-minded purpose. They won the battle tonight and six little ones are still living. It was a good day.

Dear one, I've been in hell and heaven all in one day and it hurts. Somehow I want you to know that I was a man today who lived in the middle of the whirlwind. My name was called and what I did was bad and good. You more than anyone in this world know that I am both. Pray for these refugees, pray for those who help and pray for me that I will not lose my way in this place that must break the heart of God.

All my love as always,
Dave

Generosity by itself won't save the world, but along with its contribution to human care for those who suffer, it is a sign, a reminder that we are more than our lowest common denominator. There is satisfaction in catching the next breath, eating the next meal and staying in a shelter that is protected from the elements. What makes us human are the acts of kindness: giving the cup of water, providing the way to medical care and doing what's required with an extra measure of human touch and generosity.

My experience in Zaire was a twisted, inverted experience of my humanity and others' humanity as well. My failure and helplessness led me to go deeper than ever before in my life. I found grace, the determination not to give up and the maturity to move from my own failure to help those in the valley of the shadow of death. No one can walk this path and remain unaffected. This second letter was the beginning of my coming out.

31 July 1994

Dear Diane,

My previous letter to you was heavy and full of struggle. I believe there was truth in it, but perhaps less grace than there should have been. You know that one of my favourite books is *Saint Maybe* by Anne Tyler. One of the main characters has his faith in God and himself restored in the context of a little storefront church called "The Church of the Second Chance." The words "second chance" are filled with images of grace for me. Let me explain what I mean.

On my last day at Mugunga Camp, it was time to leave. However, there, next to the vehicle, was a man lying on a stretcher. He was emaciated and feeble. No one appeared to represent his needs as we prepared to leave, so I stopped and knelt down next to him with our translator, Shavu Elias. We were unable to discover any further details about this man's case.

The medical tent was not too far away, so I contacted one of the overworked staff who graciously consented to find a place for this man. Another aid worker joined me and we carried the stretcher into the tent clinic, which was a grimy, stench-filled atmosphere. Various patients were crammed in like sardines, entangled in drips, body fluids and excrement. It was disgusting, but it was our only option. We were directed to lay the man in a small gap in the line of bodies. The medical worker had no idea where the stretcher had come from, so we left, propping it up against the tent wall.

We returned to the vehicle where everyone was waiting, but I noticed a figure on the opposite side; it was another man. Shavu spoke with the man who said, "My friends brought me here, but then left. Now I am too weak to get any closer to the tent, so I cannot get noticed." After pausing for a moment, I retrieved a water bottle from the car, gave it to him and walked back to the tent and retrieved the stretcher. Gently, we rolled the man onto the stretcher and carried him in front of the crowd. The water had roused his spirits, so that he was half sitting by the time we left.

Two second chances all at the end of the day, and one amazing opportunity yet to come. I had decided to make a last visit to Kibumba Camp, which is considered the worst of the various sites because of the terrain and the tens of thousands of people. It could be described as a moonscaped version of the last days.

We were driving north on an open flat plain with an unobstructed view. Just ahead some 500 metres was a waif-like figure tottering along next to the highway. The little arms and legs were like matchsticks. It was a little child walking into oblivion. We brought the vehicle to a halt and Shavu got out of the car and cautiously approached the child. A conversation began and we could hear a tiny voice that was delicate and precise in the local language. The figure was a little boy of six or seven perhaps; his name was Gasore. He explained that his parents had died in the forest some days ago and he survived by finding a bush to sleep in, however no one would give him any water.

After Shavu convinced us that the little fellow
had nowhere to go, we picked him up and put
him in the vehicle. I passed him my water bottle
and he proceeded to drown himself with great
gulps, spluttering and coughing as his ravished
thirst drove him to drink. We decided it was too
late to take him to the Unaccompanied Children's Centre, so we took him to our rented
house. We wrapped him in a blanket and gave
him a small portion of rice and beans. As I write
this he is in the back room sound asleep. A little
boy without hope has found some and in God's
economy we were the ministering angels. And in
my modest theologizing it was another example
of the second-chance grace of God at work.

We will fail, but always there are these second
chances to be the person that deep down you
want to be. It's not an act of penance; rather it's
the repetition of doing what you know to be
right, and then cultivating a habit that bears fruit.
Others will suffer the consequences of our fail-
ures and shortcomings. The Rwanda refugees are
simply one contemporary example of people
who are suffering from what has been done to
them as well as what they have done to others.
This is a deep mystery in the heart of God that I
don't understand. Yet more and more I believe it

is the truth. Our challenge is to look for the second chances that will reveal who we really are and glorify the God who sees evil and tragedy as an opportunity to do good.

It has been a good last day. One that I will remember for the rest of my life. This time my name was called and I answered.

All my love,

Dave

Practising generosity and compassion is a calling, not simply a set of rules or guidelines that makes our behaviour a little better. A calling reaches into the deepest part of ourselves and invites us to connect our aspirations with the deep needs of those around us. Our desire for kinship and solidarity is a reflection of the moral and spiritual order that forms the backdrop to what we touch and feel. Those who deny others generosity and compassion also deny themselves the opportunity to build a life of healthy relationships and the overwhelming joy of seeing failure turn into progress.

"Don't really have the courage to stand where I
must stand. Don't really have the temperament
to lend a helping hand."

(from "The Land of Plenty"
by Leonard Cohen and Sharon Robinson)

Chapter Eleven

The Power of Generosity: How to Get It

In October 1969 in Pasadena, California, I was a graduate student on my way to a peace march when generosity took hold of my life in a new way. As a group of us made our way through the crowd we noticed an older man in ragged clothes hustling people for small change. Even in a peace march, most folks prefer not to spend time with someone who is unshaven, unwashed and unkempt.

Without giving it much thought, I stopped along

with a couple of my friends and began speaking with this fellow. He said his name was Jim and he was no slouch in quickly discovering that he had fresh possibilities for a handout from a group of well-intentioned but naive graduate theological students. We invited him back to our house on campus, and gave him a hamburger and a soft drink. Between mouthfuls Jim told a sad story of a broken family, alcoholism and failure. There wasn't an extra bed to be had, so we put him on the couch.

Over the next few days, Jim entered into life with us, taking off during the day and coming back at night. Things came to a crisis about three days later when Jim showed up mid-evening, drunk to his socks and abusive. Being good theological students we were in the midst of our daily prayers when Jim decided to participate. However his version of praying was filled with expletives and attacks on various members of our little household. Finally, I responded, took Jim by the arm and walked him out the door, explaining that he was welcome to join us but he couldn't rage at us during our prayer time. Jim muttered some more expletives at me and then tottered off down the street.

In a "post-mortem" with my housemates we tried to sort out how Jim had managed to get his hands on so much booze. One of my friends said, "This place is starting to smell like a cheap booze factory." After a little investigation, we discovered that Jim had managed to hide bottles of cheap Tokay wine in a number of dresser drawers. Evidently he had worked out a way to maintain a private stash always at the ready. We probably weren't the first seminary house to struggle with an alcoholic in our midst, but we likely set a new precedent as part of the supply chain for an enterprising tippler.

Jim disappeared and then showed up some weeks later, repentant and further down on his luck. We gave him the expected sermon of living by the rules. It lasted for a few days until he showed up one night plastered out of his mind and asked to use our washroom. We agreed with some hesitation; we couldn't imagine that Jesus would refuse someone the use of the toilet. Jim disappeared into the washroom, which was a very small room with only a sink and a stool. All was peaceful; in fact, too peaceful. We knocked on the closed door. No response, other than an occasional groan. Finally, after repeated attempts, we managed to open the door a crack to discover that Jim had gone into a major delirium tremens episode. It was a severe reaction to his heavy drinking. Hardly conscious, he had fallen off the toilet and was jammed between it and the wall with his feet wedged against the door. He was immobilized, hardly conscious and of course totally uncooperative.

After about fifteen minutes of prying and pushing we managed to get the door open enough so that I could crawl into the washroom, lift Jim back on the toilet and open the door. Since his delirium tremens appeared to be getting worse we put him in our car and raced to the hospital. It appeared that he was a regular visitor, so we were encouraged to leave after checking on his condition. Much to our surprise Jim showed up back at our residence within an hour or so of our returning. He clearly had the inside track on how to manipulate the system. As might be expected, he was not a happy camper. He told each of us off and then turned on his heel and marched down the street.

Some months later I received a letter from Jim that had been sent by a pastor. There was no return address, only a simple apology from Jim and how he was determined to change his life. I never heard from him again. No happy ending.

I learned a number of important lessons. First, generosity isn't offered on the basis of results. Offering help is more about doing it than planning it. Second, generosity is sometimes a risky business. It takes you places you don't want to go. As a some-what naive fellow from the country, I was ripe for a hustler, but I still believe I did the right thing. Third, even when it fails, generosity feels pretty good. Helping another human being is good. Fourth, human nature is set in its ways, so don't think you can necessarily see change quickly or even any change at all. Fifth, generosity is as much about the giver as it is about the receiver. I needed to practise the generosity as much as Jim needed to receive it. In my opinion we were both beneficiaries.

So how do we get generosity? It begins with vulnerability and an openness to relate to the experiences of others. Our view moves from our micro world to the world of someone else. We are walking in someone else's shoes even though it may be just for an instant. At that time in my life, I was influenced by the idea to take more of a servant attitude toward others. How could I be helpful? Though I was aware of this concept of service, seeing Jim wandering the street prompted me to put the idea in action.

As I'm writing this chapter, it's the Christmas season. Every day there is mention in the newspaper of acts of kindness: a church is helping a visitor from a Third World country obtain an artificial leg; a group has decided to build a new home for a family that has no hope of getting one. For all the commercialism of Christmas, it is still the time of year when the public is sensitized to giving to others. Charities and churches receive the highest percentage of their contributions at Christmas. The end of the tax year plays a role in this as well.

We get the idea of generosity because it's all around us if we are prepared to look. The experience of giving opens us to others. Oseola McCarty, from Mississippi, was eighty-six when arthritis forced her to stop her lifetime career as a washerwoman. She had quit school in the sixth grade because her family needed the small income that she could provide. Her life was God, her work and her family. Oseola would work into the early hours of the morning to complete her ironing. She always walked to do her errands and she put whatever she could in her savings account.

Facing the challenges of old age, Oseola's friends encouraged her to plan for any required special medical care and for passing on her property following her death. During these planning sessions she expressed her wishes to give money to her family and to her church. And then, to the surprise of many, Oseola indicated that she wanted to give some money to the local university, the University of Southern Mississippi. Bank officials consulted with her attorney and she signed an irrevocable trust. In the following year her gift was publicly announced.

To the shock of officials and the wider world, this washerwoman with a limited education had managed to save $280,000 and she was giving $150,000 to the university. Her lack of education failed to diminish her commitment to provide an education for others. Oseola said, "I am proud that I worked hard and that my money will help young people who have worked hard to deserve it. I'm proud that I am leaving something positive in this world. My only regret is that I didn't have more to give."[1]

So how do we get generosity? How did Oseola get it? Her view of life and her place in it provided a map for her behaviour. Her sense of responsibility beginning with her own actions provided the direction. In her words, "Some people make a lot of noise about what's wrong with the world, and they are usually blaming somebody else. I think people who don't like the way things are need to look at themselves first. They need to get right with God and change their own ways. That way, they will know that they are making a difference in at least one life. If everybody did that, we'd be all right."[2]

These words may appear overly private and individualistic, but they reflect a healthy appreciation that giving to others is problematic if you are looking for someone to blame. Each of us begins with our own history. As an African American, Oseola faced many of life's trials, but she chose to practise diligence and generosity, and to leave a legacy for the next generation. Generosity doesn't require sainthood, even though an example such as Oseola's appears that way.

The desire to own things is part of our DNA. Without it we wouldn't have the energy to provide for our families, look after our children properly or take the necessary precautions to prepare for the future. Yet owning things can get way out of control.

Professor Robert C. Roberts of Baylor University describes the preoccupation with things as "a disordered desire for wealth."[3] It's the desire for unbridled acquisitiveness. We want it all. Everything else takes second place in the mad hunt to gain more wealth and possessions. This pursuit takes on the quality of covetousness—the desire for what rightfully belongs to someone else. The vulnerability and empathy for others that generosity requires is overwhelmed by this selfish affliction of wanting more, more, and more. We focus on ourselves, only to discover that when we think we have it all, the emptiness remains.

Oseola McCarty's example also demonstrates the important connection between humility and generosity. To think less of one's self rather than more is a helpful way to approach people. It opens us to see that the person who needs a hand is closer to us than we realize. Humility is an attitude that requires us to look honestly at our shortcomings and inadequacies, to be open to our own need for improvement and transformation. Humility also reflects the idea that there is something bigger than ourselves. It may be our commitment to God, to a higher ideal or a greater purpose in life.

Athletic competition can be a demonstration of generosity that pursues something greater than winning. The 1936 Olympics in Germany gives a stunning example of what it means to put generosity ahead of winning. At the height of Hitler's determination to showcase the Aryan race as superior, one event took on heightened significance. The African American Jesse Owens had already won the 100-metre dash and had run two record-breaking heats in the 200 metres. The long jump had always been considered his best event. Yet after fouls on his first two jumps, he was in danger of being disqualified. His main competitor was Germany's Luz Long, a tall, blond, blue-eyed athlete, the epitome of Hitler's racist theories. Seeing Owens' difficulties, Long approached his opponent, introduced himself and said, using American slang, "What's eating you? You should be able to qualify with your eyes closed." Long suggested that Owens mark his takeoff point a few inches in front of the board. Owens easily qualified on the next jump.

Later in the day, during the finals, Long had tied Owens at 25'10" on Owens' fifth jump. Owens cleared 26' on his next jump and then reached 26'5½" on his final jump—a new Olympic record.

In his account of this great event, sportswriter Ron Fimrite offers this description: "After the long jump competition, in which Long held on to win the silver, Owens and Long walked arm-in-arm away from the landing pit. They did not see each other after the Berlin Games, but they continued to correspond. After Long was killed in Italy during World War II, Owens faithfully kept in touch with his family.

"Before he died of lung cancer at 66 in 1980, Owens wrote: 'You can melt down all the medals and cups I have and they wouldn't be plating on the 24-carat friendship I felt for Luz Long.'"[4]

How do you get generosity? Sometimes it's a small thing that takes on rather momentous proportions. Luz Long made a small gesture that became part of a watershed moment in de-bunking a racist philosophy that took millions of lives in the coming years. His gesture was disloyal to Hitler and likely to cost Long severely, yet he did it. While an Olympic record was established, it is the generosity that is timeless.

When generosity goes against the status quo, there is a significant risk involved. Luz Long risked his future as well as his opportunity to win an Olympic championship. His payoff was simply the satisfaction of doing the right thing. Practitioners of generosity believe the world—or at least their world—will be a better place if they follow their desires to give and share. Cultivating this inner direction to be generous is an essential element of anyone wanting to develop his or her generosity habit.

It's one thing to practise generosity by giving away something that is yours, but what about situations that take away our loved ones? Can generosity be practised in moments of great personal tragedy? A parent who loses a child faces an incredible challenge, yet I'm amazed at the courage and generous nature that some parents demonstrate. Leiah Vickery Hampson was fourteen years old when she contracted encephalitis and was dead within a matter of weeks. The anguish and despair of her family and friends was almost overwhelming. Yet in the midst of all the emotional turmoil and conflicted feelings, Laura Hampson, Leiah's mother, penned these thoughts as part of the funeral tribute.

About Miracles

A lot of people have been praying for a
  miracle
That despite all odds, Leiah would survive
And that we all would have another chance
To be better parents, aunts, uncles, sisters,
  cousins and friends.
Miracles are funny things; they're not always
  what they seem.
Sort of like praying for one thing and getting
  another.
We feel like saying, "I'm sorry God. You got it
  wrong. I didn't ask for THAT."
Well, God's ways are not ours. I take comfort
  in believing that the more the ways of this
  world make sense to us, the further away we
  are from what really makes sense.
I believe that a lot of miracles *have* occurred
  over the past several weeks.
I'm certain that despite the physical manifesta-
  tions of Leiah's disease she felt at peace
  inside.
Although she could not speak to us
Her spirit did hear all the loving words
Feel all the caring touches
And gloried in the many heartfelt prayers.

Leiah was a gift to us, one we neither deserved
    nor paid for
She was never ours to own, only ours to care
    for and enjoy.
As a mother my wish is that Leiah's legacy
    would be this:
That all parents ensure that their children
    know they are cherished,
Beyond any job, material possession or other
    distraction
So that every night each child can go to bed
    knowing how much he or she is loved
In spite of any disagreements or harsh words
    that might have preceded bedtime
So that if that day were to be their last
That child would be able to say he or she felt
    loved.
Because that's all that really matters.[5]

In the traumatic mystery of her daughter's death,
Laura Hampson writes with a generous spirit and
an overflowing heart. Her desire to be positive,
thankful and caring marks her as a generous person
of the highest order. Laura's humility before one of
life's greatest losses was sustained by her personal
faith in God, and her daughter's life was a gift rather

than something she possessed. Upon the departure of this gift, Laura was prepared to see the joy of the time together rather than the despair of the time that would never be. Her generous view of life is a compelling testimony to the difference that generosity can make. Getting generosity goes to the very depths of our soul and expressing it in the challenges and deepest tragedies of life sets an example that others will seek to follow.

"You must be the change you wish to see in
the world."

(Mahatma Gandhi)

Chapter Twelve

The Power of Generosity in a World of Change

Generosity is challenged by the global barriers between us. These are the issues that separate us from each other, even though we live in an Internet world that claims to offer connectivity for everyone. Living in the twenty-first century offers tremendous opportunities to those who have, but for the three billion people of the world living on less than two dollars a day it's a crushing existence of grinding poverty, despair and unremitting daily challenges. Being generous in this kind of world is a critical element in making the world safer and better for everyone, but the barriers are growing.

The disparity between rich and poor is immense. Even though low-income countries are seeing some growth in their economies, high-income countries still dominate. With high-income countries controlling about 80 percent of the world's Gross Domestic Product, wealth will remain in the hands of the wealthy unless something changes. [1]

To use a travel metaphor, the poor are walking on foot while the affluent are flying an airplane in pursuit of the same destination. At this rate the poor will never arrive. We can make a Darwinian choice that leaves the poor neglected and marginalized or we can respond with genuine care and compassion that seeks access and opportunity for the world's most disadvantaged peoples.

On a trip to northern Kenya, East Africa, I was visiting a village where the people were walking five kilometres every day in the hot sun to draw water from a riverbed. They would dig down about six metres and wait for the water to seep into the bottom of the hole. Earlier in my travels I read an article that explained how Coca Cola's goal was to have a bottle of Coke within an arm's reach of every person on the face of the earth. Coke is making faster progress in pursuit of its vision than many poor communities in obtaining safe drinking water. There is something incredibly wrong with this.

The HIV/AIDS crisis is wreaking havoc in Africa and threatening to exercise the same destruction in other parts of the world, such as China and India. Infection rates are moving slowly but steadily upward. The impact is profound. Unless things change there will be twenty-five million orphans in Africa by the year 2010—that means children raised without parents, with minimal education, and trapped by poverty. Authorities estimate that development is slipping backward at an astounding pace. In Zambia, the average life span for adult men has dropped from over fifty to thirty-eight years in the last decade, and it's still declining.

So many adults have died of AIDS that crops aren't being planted and harvested. In high-infection countries, schoolteachers are dying faster than governments can replace them. Grandparents have become the guardians and parents of their grandchildren because their own children have died of AIDS. The havoc on the social systems is difficult to grasp. The particularly insidious nature of AIDS is the way it destroys the most productive part of the population, killing those between eighteen and forty-five and leaving behind the children and grandparents.

With HIV/AIDS, sexual violence and abuse levelled against teenage girls is increasing. Men see girls as less likely to be HIV-positive, so they demand sexual favours with money and coercion. The girls come from poverty so the money offered is the only way to feed their families.

Even before AIDS, women and girls were the most discriminated part of the population in all poor countries. They are least likely to be educated, the last to be fed and then sent off to an early marriage. Is it possible for any society to truly develop when half its population is routinely discriminated against and marginalized? Women are the nurturers and the primary food providers in many countries. If this barrier is allowed to continue, the likelihood of development is diminished in many poor countries.

Young men are increasingly violent in poor countries because they have little hope for their future. A young man in Yemen was asked whether he was going to school. He replied: "Why do I need to go to school when I have a gun?" This is the generation that will be coming to power over the next decade. A study from Toronto's York University demonstrates that countries with young populations, and particularly with many young, poor males, are more subject to political violence. In short, a society with too many young, violence-prone males who have no jobs or future prospects can expect desperate behaviours that wreak havoc on society.[2] The violence in Sierra Leone and the Democratic Republic of the Congo is tied directly to the lack of adequate income, the prevailing government corruption and a civil society in tatters.

The conventions of everyday civility fall apart when young men schooled in the most violent behaviour take to the streets. Violence becomes an expression of their hurts and disappointments, with chaos and moral anarchy the result. Michael Ignatieff, in his book *The Warrior's Honour*, describes how the restraints and codes of honour for soldiers are eroded as various factions and groups take to the streets.[3] The line between soldier and civilian is blurred, and the willingness to use any means to wreak havoc is ominous and frightening.

The recent intervention in Iraq revealed coalition forces struggling with the dual but conflicting goals of conducting a military assault and protecting civilians. At times the military restraint was unusual, with soldiers allowing civilians to move freely, even to the point where soldiers absented themselves from religious shrines. Yet, at other times, sophisticated military technology struck military targets and civilians with equal force. Whole families were obliterated, footnotes on the march to victory in a very complex environment. With the benefit of hindsight it's apparent that Iraq's capabilities to fight were vastly over-rated, including the estimates of its weapons of mass destruction. The coalition forces were far more than a match for this weakened and inferior foe. The use of drone aircraft and sophisticated technological weapons against foot soldiers makes the mismatch even more dramatic. To those in poor countries who are both repelled and attracted by the superiority of affluent countries, and especially of the United States, this kind of fighting appears both unfair and dishonourable. The resulting dilemma highlights the complexity of intervention even for the best of reasons.

The disparity of the marketplace is a major issue as well. While Western countries preach a free market philosophy, the world's poor countries know from bitter experience that the market is not free. In most situations they can't even get to the market table. At times it appears that Western countries would rather dole out foreign aid than enable the poor countries to become trading partners. There is a powerful tension in the First World countries that want to protect their economies while paying lip service to increasing the opportunities for poor countries to participate in the global economy.

At the local community level I have visited families who have no source of capital other than loans with ridiculously high interest rates, procured on the black market. It becomes another cycle of poverty for families who borrow small amounts of money at interest rates as high as 100 percent over the course of a few months. Most are unable to pay it back, so they borrow more. Often the result is the selling of their children into bonded labour to pay back the loan plus interest. The payback may go on year after year.

In his book *The Mystery of Capital*, Peruvian economist Hernando de Soto argues that if the poor squatting on land had proper ownership, they would have the collateral to obtain the small loans that could revolutionize their opportunities and lifestyle. He estimates that the total value of the real estate held but not owned by the poor of the Third World and former communist countries is at least $9.3 trillion. De Soto further calculates that 80 percent of the world is undercapitalized.[4]

I have visited families in various poor countries where the opportunity to obtain a loan as small as thirty dollars at a reasonable interest rate changes their situation dramatically. With a little training in bookkeeping and elementary marketing they can start small businesses such as tailoring, handcrafts, vegetable gardens, poultry and carpentry. The result is increased income that provides basic health care, education, proper shelter and food for the family. Mothers and fathers who lived never knowing where the next meal might come from now have small businesses that restore the health of their families while building dignity and self-reliance.

Perhaps the greatest issue that divides our world is the growing isolation of those who have from those who don't. This unfortunate reality is true in Western societies as well. In Canada the numbers of hungry children have grown over the last decade. The latest statistics indicate that one in six children in Canada live in poverty, in a country that has frequently been described as one of the best places to live in the world.

In Canada we are also facing the challenges of a society that is increasingly a tapestry of different races, ethnicities and religions. Ignoring each other and hoping for the best is not an adequate response. The challenge is to respect our differences while finding the common values that hold us together as communities and countries. In fact, Canada has a continuing opportunity to set an example for the world. Some of our cities have a mix of people that is as diverse and varied as anywhere.

Generosity is an important part of an effective response to the barriers that restrict and fragment our world. There is a call for justice, equity and opportunity as well, but a generous attitude offers a point of beginning for the many actions required. Businesses are expressing a growing awareness of social responsibility. In Canada the Imagine program encourages businesses to give a minimum of one percent of their after-tax profits to charities that are addressing the needs of society. Increasingly, businesses are aware that they have an important stake in the well-being of society if they are to be profitable over the long haul.

At a personal level, there are more people interested in seeing first-hand the situations of human need in the world. World Vision's Destination Life Change program is involving scores of people in overseas orientation and work experiences. Organizations such as Habitat for Humanity see growing numbers of people prepared to get involved. Volunteering continues to be on the increase. While the latest statistics in Canada show that volunteering has decreased from 31 percent of the population in 1997 to 27 percent in 2000, those who are volunteering have increased their average hours from 149 to 162 during the same period.[5] People with wealth and influence are recognizing their obligation to contribute to a healthier country and world in significant ways. There is something to be said for doing good while doing well.

The World Bank, as the primary international financial system, is showing signs of self-criticism and review that are extremely important. There is an acknowledgment that structural adjustment during the 1980s required many poor countries to pay too high a price. In efforts to reduce their debt load and overhaul their financial structures, they were forced to diminish their social services in health care and education. The result was devastating for the very poor and the re-structuring was largely ineffective in addressing the economic challenges of the country. In response, the World Bank is taking a more thoughtful approach in combining the responsibility to address poverty with economic strategies that give disadvantaged countries a place at the marketplace of nations. Yet it remains to be seen if the initiatives are profound enough to bring about the changes that will really help poor countries.

Generosity is still only one of many responses required to address the challenges of our world. To be generous is to open the door to new possibilities.

Without this attitude we resign ourselves to the restraints that keep us locked in the status quo. Our hope for the future rests with those who see possibilities and who contribute to the solution with personal commitment, creativity and hard work. We all have a choice—to be part of the problem or part of the solution. The generosity journey is far from over, but there are encouraging signs that the way ahead offers hope and new beginnings.

Appendix A

How to Be a More Generous Person: 5 Steps Forward

1. Work on the inside

Being a more generous person is an inside job. It needs to flow from who you want to become. You will need a foundation for this change in your life. Why do you want to be more generous? It may be your religious faith, your personal philosophy or the values that you hold to be self-evident. Generosity is not about following a command. It needs to be a reflection of your deepest motivations.

Find a group of people that shares your commitment and interest. It may be a church or a club. Search for a group of kindred spirits who are prepared to look at issues and opportunities addressing lifestyle and concern for others. I meet every Tuesday morning with six other men who encourage and challenge one another to practise our faith at the highest level.

Read books and magazines that address the deeper issues of life. There are some wonderful books that tell stories of generous people. Generosity emerges out of commitments to serve others.

Inspirational books and literature offer a wonderful way to end your day. Going to sleep with positive, encouraging thoughts about how life can be transformed and renewed gives "power sleep." Try it. I used to think it was a manipulative gimmick, but it really does make a difference. Obviously there are going to be times when your reading at the end of the day will be less than inspiring, but try this positive approach.

2. Polish up your attitude

Generous people usually have more positive attitudes because they have discovered it's hard to be generous toward others if you are negative. Most people will respond in an affirming way if they are approached by a positive person.

When you are thinking about people, especially those you work with, look at the possibilities they have. Seeing potential in someone else means that you will likely see more potential in yourself too. Approach life expecting some good things to happen. Our founder at World Vision used to talk about leaving "God room" in our plans and activities. He was referring to the likelihood that divine intervention would make our best even better. If that's too religious for you, then think of it as "serendipity room." Good surprises will happen.

Slow down. Take time to appreciate the people around you. By paying attention to them you will be paying attention to your own need to relate to others. What most people appreciate more than anything else is being noticed. They are on our agenda. Someone cares enough to listen.

Practise gratitude. Life gives us more than we are owed, and we need to see it as a gift. Gratitude turns a negative attitude into a positive one. Being thankful enables us to give more away because we are confident that more will continue to flow our way.

3. Cultivate some generosity habits

Look for chances to be an encourager. You can't encourage someone unless you are willing to share some of your time and perspective. Generosity flows out of encouragement—or maybe it's the other way around. Take time to thank or acknowledge someone doing a routine task. Sometimes when we are the recipients of such encouragement we can see the benefits of our efforts even more clearly.

Recently I was passing through the security system at the international airport in Hawaii. Carelessly, I had left a small Swiss Army knife in my carry-on bag. At the security point, the officer identified the item and told me they would have to confiscate it. My first reaction was irritation, but then I realized it was my own forgetfulness. In the meantime the agent approached and expressed his regret, since the knife is something of value. Next, to my amazement, he offered to mail it to me. I was speechless. I offered to give him a couple of dollars for postage, but he quickly said that wasn't necessary. He handed me his business card, which included the name of his supervisor. A few days after returning to Toronto, my knife appeared in the mail and I sent off a note expressing my appreciation. A gesture of generosity had turned a routine disappointment around because someone was prepared to be helpful beyond the call of duty.

Smile—be open. It's truly amazing how seldom people acknowledge each other with a simple smile. In public places, you have a harvest field of opportunity to give someone a lift emotionally. It's my experience that the most neglected members of the public are those who do the routine public services—the janitor, the server, the attendant and the clerk. People are as hungry for a smile as for a good meal.

A simple "thank you" for a service given is also a relationship opener. My own awareness was challenged in a new way when our daughter worked as a waitress. The rude and ungrateful behaviour of patrons was shocking. It has changed my attitude when I go to restaurants.

Acknowledge people who are immigrants or of a different ethnic group. In insidious little ways, society pushes us to socialize exclusively with those who are like ourselves. We can stand against that by making contact with those who are different from us.

Business writer Michael Zigarelli describes a little gimmick he has developed to cultivate generosity. "Place four or five coins in your right pocket at the beginning of each day and then move one coin to the left pocket each time you compliment, praise or encourage someone during the work day. Don't leave work until all the coins are in your left pocket. As you get better at this, increase the number of coins you start with each day." Zigarelli explains that some people are natural encouragers, but he is not. He doesn't think about it. His coin approach reminds him to make this a priority.

In a survey of 300 leaders and their praise behaviour, Zigarelli found that most offered praise to an employee only about once a week. Women appear to be more generous with praise than men.[1] The opportunity for improvement is staggering.

Learn to say "I'm sorry" sooner rather than later. Harbouring self-justification can be toxic, especially when we have harmed someone else. "I am sorry" are three of the most powerful words in the English language. Use them liberally. They will change you and those around you more quickly than almost anything else. By taking the initiative, you will find that the other person involved is likely to acknowledge his or her responsibility as well.

4. Share what you have

Look for opportunities to share your time, expertise and finances so that others may benefit. Look for some good causes that address the pressing needs of people. Whether rich or poor, you have something that can encourage and benefit others. Look in your neighbourhood as well as overseas. In the next section I have identified some criteria that will help you determine what makes a good charity to support. But first you need to decide what causes attract or interest you. Does someone in your family suffer from a particular medical or health-related condition? Find a charity that addresses that need. If you have a family, you may want to choose a charity that offers a chance for your children to get involved. I have a number of friends who have taken their children on a brief trip overseas to help build a school, a church or houses. Their lives, and their children's, will never be the same.

There are many opportunities here in Canada. Volunteering for food banks, soup kitchens, school activities, drop-in centres or faith-related activities are just some examples. Helping with a home building project here in Canada is also a creative way to get family members and neighbours involved.

Activities like this enable you to build some "service memories" with your family. One of my friends describes how a family Christmas trip to Mexico to help build a house is something his children will never forget. In fact, the children enjoyed it so much that they went back the next Christmas as well.

Determine a percentage of your income that you can give away by investing in others. Previously I've mentioned 10 percent, but choose what you can give with enthusiasm. You can help meet the immediate life-threatening needs of someone as well as invest in charity work that tackles the root causes of illness, poverty, injustice and diminished hope. Money is a measure of what really matters to you. How you spend it is connected to your expression of generosity.

5. Learn what makes you tick

What are your strengths when it comes to expressing concern and encouragement to others? Where do you draw your energy? What motivates your most significant behaviours? Understanding yourself will help you determine what is the right path for you. There are numerous diagnostic tools that are fun and practical. Tests such as the Myers-Briggs Type Indicator, a version of this called True Colours, and a seminar called Life Keys can help you find your way. These different approaches will identify your strengths and weaknesses while making connections with your dreams and expectations. Many organizations and businesses have tools like this in their Human Resource area. Take some initiative to seek some professional help. Most organizations will be delighted that you asked. Local churches often have access to these resources as well.

Being more generous is not a panacea. The challenges you currently have will likely remain, but you may discover that you can make something more of the gifts and resources you already have. Self-help often attracts some criticism because it can be superficial and manipulative. Yet in my own experience I have discovered that many changes for good in the world began with someone saying, "I'm not satisfied with the way things are." Whether it's overcoming addictions, striving for a higher level of performance, improving the lives of our families, addressing deep issues of injustice or experiencing profound spiritual growth, someone has to say, "I want to change." My hope for you is that a commitment to greater generosity will make your life better and the world better as well. It's never too late. No time is better than now!

Appendix B

What's a Great Charity?

Many factors combine to make a great charity. Good programs are necessary, along with staff, a board of directors and management who are prepared to pursue excellence at every level. People make the difference. Here are some suggestions to help you identify great charities:

1. People of passion and commitment

Does the organization really believe in what it's doing? Great organizations reflect an enthusiasm that is energetic and contagious. The staff is knowledgeable about the organization and they are prepared to explain the mission and the work that is taking place. Compelling organizations have staff who view their work as a calling rather than a job. They can describe the mission of the charity with understanding and clarity. If your life was on the line, is this the kind of organization you would want in your corner?

2. People who do what they say

After you have made your donation, do you see evidence that it has been spent in the way you intended? Does the charity provide an annual report? If you ask for their complete audited financial statements, do they provide them in a timely fashion? Great organizations respond to the requests of their supporters with tact, promptness and thoroughness.

3. People who put their supporters first

Great charities know they are servants to those who care. They are a channel of outreach and concern, with an attitude to serve those who receive, but also those who give. Your personal information needs to be treated confidentially. Names should never be traded or given to other charities without your permission. Supporters should have a say in how often they will be solicited. All of the communication you receive should respect your dignity and the dignity of the beneficiaries.

4. People who practise responsible governance and oversight

Great charities are governed by boards of directors who take their job very seriously. They are volunteers who serve without pay because they believe in the cause. The names of the directors should be readily available to the public. Part of their role is to ensure that a respected and certified accounting firm audits the organization annually.

Great organizations control their costs so that maximum funds are directed to program work while ensuring that management pursues growth in support and volunteers. They meet or exceed the legal requirements of charities mandated by federal and provincial legislation, and their boards ensure that they fulfill the financial reporting required by Canada Revenue Agency. They are accountable to an external group that sets industry standards and a code of ethics.

5. People who don't promise more than they can deliver

Most charities are involved in activities that require long-term assistance and development work. There are no quick fixes. Great charities acknowledge the complexity of the task while expressing their satisfaction that they are moving forward in the right direction. They demonstrate a practical approach that shows measurable and verifiable results. The people who benefit from the charity's activities should be given a voice and representation in the process. There is a clear effort to avoid paternalism and dependency.

Some might suggest that using language like being a "great charity" is a sign of arrogance. Indeed it might be argued that no charity can claim to be great. I beg to differ. Charities need to set the bar higher if they intend to improve their performance. Pursuing greatness in the name of important causes that will save and enrich lives needs no apology. In a world where the voices of greed and self-centredness grow daily, the pursuit of great charities is an antidote that offers hope for the future.

Appendix C

Am I Greedy?

Most of us are a bit generous and a bit greedy, and our attitudes may fluctuate from day to day. Few of us are so generous as to have no need of improvement (although St. Francis and Mother Teresa come to mind).

To help you focus your own self-examination, answer the following questions. The questionnaire is a rough measure of your generosity. The questions provide only a generous and a greedy option. The import of the answer given may vary with the circumstances of the one giving the answer. The point is not to rate yourself, but to help you learn to become more generous.

Appendix C

1. *If I fantasize about winning a magazine sweepstakes, what most comes to mind is:* (a) what I could do for others with all that money; (b) what I could buy, the vacations I could take, and the freedom to do what I want.

2. *When I hear of someone with about the same talents and energy and education as I have who earns $20,000 a year more than I do, I think:* (a) how nice that he or she can earn that much money; (b) it's not fair.

3. *When someone outside my family gives me a significant gift out of the blue:* (a) I feel good about being the recipient of someone's generosity, and am comfortable with remaining in his or her "debt"; (b) I refuse it, or if I accept it I feel uncomfortable until I have given the giver something of equal or greater value.

4. *If I express my admiration for some possession of an acquaintance (a book, a painting, a piece of pottery), and the acquaintance offers to give it to me, I tend to think:* (a) "This person is very generous"; (b) "What do you suppose he or she wants from me?"

5. *When I give someone a gift:* (a) I am content if the person acknowledges the gift with pleasure; (b) I feel cheated if the person doesn't pretty

soon do me a favour or give me a gift of equal or greater value.

6. *When I give money to my place of worship or to a charitable organization, I typically:* (a) think with pleasure about the good that may be done with my money; (b) think of the things I could have done with the money if I hadn't given it away.

7. *If I lend $15 to someone I meet at a retreat or conference:* (a) I don't mind much if I never see the money again; (b) I get pretty upset if the person doesn't repay me.

8. *When I give money to my place of worship, I do so because:* (a) I like to see it doing well; (b) I feel it wouldn't be right not to give.

9. *When I get a significant raise or come into some money:* (a) it does not affect my standard of living; (b) my standard of living increases.

10. *When I get a raise or switch to a higher-income job:* (a) my feelings about myself don't change much; (b) I tend to feel very good about myself for a while, but soon I begin to feel "poor" again.

11. *When something of value is being distributed in a group—fish at the end of a fishing trip or leftover food at a picnic—if I can manage to get a bit more for myself than others without seeming greedy:* (a) I will not do it; (b) I will do it.

12. *In a situation like those described in question 11, in order not to behave greedily:* (a) I make no effort—greed does not tempt me; (b) I have to use self-control to overcome greedy impulses.

Notes

Chapter 1

1 Tibor Machan, *Generosity: Virtue in Civil Society* (Washington, D.C.: Cato Institute, 1998), 24.
2 Willard G. Oxtoby, ed., *World Religions— Western Traditions* (Toronto: Oxford University Press, 1996), 406–7.
3 Allan Luks and Peggy Payne, *The Healing Power of Doing Good* (New York: iUniverse.com, 2001).
4 Ibid., 5.
5 Irina Ratushinskaya, *Grey Is the Colour of Hope* (New York: Random House, 1989), 260.
6 Ibid., 238.

Chapter 2

1 Free the Children, www.freethechildren.org
2 Morton Hunt, *The Compassionate Beast* (New York: Doubleday, 1991), 198–209.
3 E. Stanley Jones, *Mastery* (Nashville, Tenn.: Abingdon Press, 1955), 218.
4 Lewis B. Smedes, *A Pretty Good Person* (New York: Harper and Row, 1990), 175–79.

Chapter 4

1 Gerry McCarthy, "The Pursuit of Happiness," *The Toronto Star*, 6 August 2000.
2 Leslie Ferenc, "A Real Campaign Donor," *The Toronto Star*, 29 October 2002.
3 James M. Kouzes and Barry Z. Posner, *Encouraging the Heart* (San Francisco, Cal.: Jossey-Bass, 1999), 9–11.
4 Ibid., 13.

Chapter 5

1. The Center on Philanthropy at Indiana University, *America Gives—Survey of Americans' Generosity After September 11* (The Center on Philanthropy at Indiana University, January 2002).

2. Walker Information, *Measuring the Business Value of Corporate Philanthropy* (Indianapolis: Walker Information, May 2002).

3. Mother Teresa and José Luis González-Balado. *Mother Teresa: In My Own Words*. (London: Hodder and Stoughton, 1996), 19.

Chapter 6

1. John Perkins, *Let Justice Roll Down* (Ventura, Cal.: G/L Publications, 1976).

2. Reported on *Good Morning America*, ABC Television, 30 July 2002.

3. Brennan Manning, *The Ragamuffin Gospel* (Portland, Ore.: Multnomah Press, 1990), 91–92.

Chapter 7

1 Nelson Mandela, *Long Walk to Freedom* (New York: Little, Brown, 1994), 542.

2 Ibid., 466.

3 Ibid., 542.

4 Edwin Markham, "Outwitted," *Poems of Edwin Markham* (New York: Harper and Brothers, 1950), 18.

5 Stan Mooneyham, *Dancing on the Strait and Narrow* (New York: Harper and Row, 1989), 30.

6 World Vision Archives, "Deborah's Story: A Tale of Reconciliation in Rwanda," January 2001, reported by James Wackett.

Chapter 8

1 *Baran*, Majid Majidi, dir., 1 videocassette (93 minutes), (Iran: Fouad Nahas and Majid Majidi).

Chapter 9

1 Michael Adams, *Better Happy Than Rich?* (Toronto, Ont.: Viking, 2000), 78.

Chapter 11

1 Association of Fundraising Professionals, "Simple Wisdom for Rich Living," *Advancing Philanthropy* (Winter 1996–97), 44–46.

2 Ibid., 46.

3 Robert C. Roberts, *The Sin of Greed and the Spirit of Christian Generosity* [booklet] (Center for Applied Christian Ethics, Wheaton College, 1994).

4 Ron Fimrite, "The Day Athletics Won Out Over Politics," Flashback, Olympic Daily, *Sports Illustrated*, 29 July 1996.

5 Laura Leavens Hampson, "A Service of Thanksgiving for the Life of Leiah Vickery Hampson." From eulogy given at Trinity Anglican Church, Mississauga, 29 April 1998.

Chapter 12

1 United Nations Development Program, *Human Development Report 2003* (New York: Oxford University Press, 2003).

2 Robert Kaplan, *The Coming Anarchy* (New York: Random House, 2000), 75–76, quoted in a York

University study by Christian G. Mesquite and
Neil I. Wiener.

3   Michael Ignatieff, *The Warrior's Honour* (New
York: Henry Holt and Company, 1997), 159.

4   Hernando de Soto, *The Mystery of Capital*, (New
York: Basic Books, 2000), 39–40.

5   Statistics Canada, *Highlights from the 2000
National Survey of Giving,Volunteering and
Participating*. No. 71-542-XIE.

Appendix A

1   Michael Zigarelli, interviewed in Dr. John C.
Maxwell's "Management by Encouragement,"
Leadership Wired [online newsletter], Vol. 6,
No. 6, March 2003, www.maximumimpact.
com.

Bibliography

Adams, Michael. *Better Happy Than Rich?* Toronto, Ont.: Viking, 2000.

America Gives—Survey of Americans' Generosity After September 11, The Center on Philanthropy at Indiana University, January 2002.

Association of Fundraising Professionals, "Simple Wisdom for Rich Living," *Advancing Philanthropy* (Winter 1996–97), 44–46.

Baran, Majid Majidi, dir., 1 videocassette (93 minutes), Iran: Fouad Nahas and Majid Majidi, 2001.

The Bible, New International Version, International Bible Society, 1978.

The Bible, New Revised Standard Version, National Council of the Churches of Christ in the United

States of America (Division of Christian Education), 1989.

Cohen, Leonard and Sharon Robinson, "The Land of Plenty," from *Leonard Cohen: Ten New Songs*, Columbia, 2001. Produced by Sharon Robinson.

Coles, Romand. *Rethinking Generosity*. Ithaca, NY, and London, UK: Cornell University, 1997.

Denny, Frederick Mathewson. *An Introduction to Islam*. New York: Macmillan, 1994.

de Soto, Hernando. *The Mystery of Capital*. New York: Basic Books, 2000.

Ferenc, Leslie. "A Real Campaign Donor," *The Toronto Star*, 29 October 2002.

Fimrite, Ron. "The Day Athletics Won Out Over Politics," Flashback, Olympic Daily, *Sports Illustrated*, 29 July 1996.

Free the Children, www.freethechildren.org

Good Morning America, ABC Television, 30 July 2002.

Hampson, Laura Leavens. "A Service of Thanksgiving for the Life of Leiah Vickery Hampson." From eulogy given at Trinity Anglican Church, Mississauga, 29 April 1998.

Hunt, Morton. *The Compassionate Beast*. New York: Doubleday, 1991.

Ignatieff, Michael. *The Warrior's Honor*. New York: Henry Holt and Company, 1997.

Jones, E. Stanley. *Mastery*. Nashville, Tenn.: Abingdon Press, 1955.

Kaplan, Robert. *The Coming Anarchy*. New York: Random House, 2000. Quoted in a York University study by Christian G. Mesquite and Neil I. Wiener.

Kouzes, James M. and Barry Z. Posner. *Encouraging the Heart*. San Francisco, Cal.: Jossey-Bass, 1999.

Leddy, Mary Jo. *Radical Gratitude*. Maryknoll, NY: Orbis Books, 2002.

Luks, Allan and Peggy Payne. *The Healing Power of Doing Good*. New York: iUniverse.com, 2001.

Machan, Tibor R. *Generosity: Virtue in Civil Society*. Washington, D.C.: Cato Institute, 1998.

Mandela, Nelson. *Long Walk to Freedom*. New York: Little, Brown and Company, 1994.

Manning, Brennan. *The Ragamuffin Gospel*. Portland, Ore.: Multnomah Press, 1990.

Markham, Edwin. "Outwitted." *Poems of Edwin Markham*. New York: Harper and Brothers, 1950.

McCarthy, Gerry. "The Pursuit of Happiness." *The Toronto Star*, 6 August 2000.

Mooneyham, William Stanley. *Dancing on the Strait and Narrow*. New York: Harper and Row, 1989.

Mother Teresa and José Luis González-Balado. *Mother Teresa: In My Own Words*. London: Hodder and Stoughton, 1996.

Bibliography

Oliner, Samuel P. *Do Unto Others*. Boulder, Col.:
Westview Press, 2003.

Oxtoby, Willard G. *World Religions—Western
Traditions*. Toronto: Oxford University Press,
1996.

Perkins, John. *Let Justice Roll Down*. Ventura, Cal.:
G/L Publications, 1976.

Peterson, Eugene. *The Message: The Bible in
Contemporary Language*. Colorado Springs, Col.:
NavPress Publishing Group, 1993.

The Random Acts of Kindness Foundation,
www.actsofkindness.org.

Ratushinskaya, Irina. *Grey Is the Colour of Hope*.
Translated by Alyona Kojevnikov. New York:
Alfred A. Knopf, 1988.

Roberts, Robert C. *The Sin of Greed and the Spirit of
Christian Generosity* [booklet]. Center for Applied
Christian Ethics, Wheaton College, 1994.

Roehlkepartain, Eugene C., Elanah Dalyah Naftali,
and Laura Musegades. *Growing Up Generous*.
Bethesda, Md.: The Alban Institute, 2000.

Severy, Merle, ed. *Great Religions of the World*. USA:
National Geographic Society, 1971, 1978.

Sider, Ron. *Just Generosity*. Grand Rapids, Mich.:
Baker Books, 1999.

Smedes, Lewis B. *A Pretty Good Person*. New York:
Harper and Row Publishers, 1990.

Sober, Elliott and David Sloan Wilson. *Unto Others.* Cambridge, Mass.: Harvard University Press, 1998.

Statistics Canada, *Highlights from the 2000 National Survey of Giving, Volunteering and Participating*. No. 71-542-XIE.

United Nations Development Program, *Human Development Report 2003*, New York: Oxford University Press, 2003.

Walker Information. *Measuring the Business Value of Corporate Philanthropy*. Indianapolis: Walker Information, May 2002.

World Vision Archives. *Deborah's Story: A Tale of Reconciliation in Rwanda*, January 2001. Reported by James Wackett.

Wuthnow, Robert. *Acts of Compassion*. Princeton, NJ: Princeton University Press, 1991.

Zigarelli, Michael, interviewed in Dr. John C. Maxwell's "Management by Encouragement," *Leadership Wired* [online newsletter], Vol. 6, No. 6, March 2003, www.maximumimpact.com.